CHOOSING A COLLEGE

CHOOSING A
COLLEGE

A Guide for Parents and Students

THOMAS SOWELL

PERENNIAL LIBRARY

Harper & Row, Publishers, New York
Grand Rapids, Philadelphia, St. Louis, San Francisco
London, Singapore, Sydney, Tokyo

FIRST EDITION

Designed by Joan Greenfield

Library of Congress Cataloging-in-Publication Data

Sowell, Thomas, 1930–
    Choosing a college : a guide for parents and students / Thomas Sowell. — 1st ed.
        p.   cm.
    Includes index.
    ISBN 0-06-055151-8 : $. — ISBN 0-06-096354-9 (pbk.) : $
    1. College, Choice of—United States.   2. Universities and colleges—United States—Admission.   I. Title.
LB2350.5.S64   1989
378'.1056'0973—dc19   88-46110
                                                                CIP

---

89 90 91 92 93 WG/FG 10 9 8 7 6 5 4 3 2 1
89 90 91 92 93 WG/FG 10 9 8 7 6 5 4 3 2 1 (pbk.)

To Shirley Raymer, College Admissions
Preparatory Service

CONTENTS

INTRODUCTION

With all the college guides already loading down the shelves of bookstores, what excuse can there be for publishing yet another one? This guide does not even pretend to compete with, or substitute for, those huge college guides that are chock-full of statistics about hundreds of colleges. Neither does it attempt to match the vignettes of particular colleges and universities found in some other guides.

The purpose of this book is to start you out at square one, before you even know what questions to ask, what colleges to read about, or what statistics to look up. Step by step, it builds up your knowledge of what colleges, universities, and engineering schools are all about, how and why they differ—and, most important of all, what those differences mean to you when choosing where to apply. This is a how-to-do-it book, designed to help you find the kind of college that will fit your own particular goals, ability, pocketbook, and way of life. It tells you what to look for during a campus visit, how to read a college brochure so as to get what you need to know out of it, regardless of what message the college itself is trying to send, and—at the end of the process—how to evaluate the admissions and financial aid offers that come in, before deciding where you really want to go.

In short, the purpose of this book is to help parents and students sort out some basic and very important questions that they need to do some serious thinking about—and looking into—no matter what college they are considering. Only after these fundamentals are well understood will voluminous statistics or descriptions of particular colleges have a context in which they make sense. Many of these fundamentals are surprising and some are quite disturbing.

Although this book deals in general principles, it also names names and pulls no punches in revealing what some colleges are doing—something that might be very difficult for a guide that has to go back to those same colleges next year to update their statistics. The purpose is not muckraking sensationalism, however. The purpose is to offer some practical suggestions for students and their parents. The mention of parents is not incidental, nor mere politeness. Too often those advising students see parents as an unfortunate encumbrance to be finessed aside. But if the advice leads to disaster—as happens more than a few times—it will be the parents who will have to pick up the pieces, not the confident counselors. This book hopes to put some backbone into parents who might otherwise be intimidated by "experts."

Parents should never forget that it was the educational "experts" who, with ever larger amounts of money to spend, produced a consistently declining educational product for almost two decades. Beginning in the early 1960s, the test scores of American high school students declined every year from what they were the year before, on into the late 1970s. To make matters worse, grades were going up while results were going down. Parents and the public were deceived, not only by rising grades but also by glowing rhetoric about the benefits of "innovative" education.

The deception did not end there. Once the test score decline became a national scandal, educators claimed that this decline was due to an influx of disadvantaged students whose low scores brought down the average. In reality, however, the test score decline *at the top* was especially drastic. The number of students scoring 700 or higher on the verbal S.A.T. in 1982 was less than half the number who scored that high in 1972.

On something as important as choosing a college, parents should not defer to, or be intimidated by, educators who have failed so many children in so many ways for so long. Many educators are good at smooth and lofty talk, delivered with airs of certainty and an implication that you must be very backward if you disagree or even question. But parents and students both have too much at stake to allow themselves to be led around by the nose this way. They need to get their own facts. But before that, they need to think through what facts they will need—and why. That is the purpose of this book.

Specific colleges are discussed here, not so much to convey information about those particular colleges but to illustrate general principles which might seem purely theoretical and abstract otherwise. If I go into certain differences to consider when choosing between Bennington College and Franklin & Marshall College, for example, the same principles can be useful if you have no intention of applying to either but are choosing between Evergreen State and Occidental, or between Hampshire and Lafayette colleges. If the illustrations happen to include colleges, universities, or engineering schools that you are in fact considering, so much the better. These illustrations may also suggest some institutions you were not familiar with, but which you may find worth exploring further.

The distinctions made between particular colleges, and particular kinds of colleges, are not meant to be rankings in the sense of showing who is in the "top 10" or among the academic elite, the most exclusive, or the like. What you are really looking for is a college that will be best for one individual. If this book helps you to sort out the kinds of things to take into account to find that college for yourself, it will have served its purpose.

PART I:

WHAT TO CONSIDER

CHAPTER 1

AN IMPORTANT DECISION

Choosing a college is often the second most important decision in life—exceeded only by the choice of a wife or a husband. In money terms, college can easily be the second largest expenditure in life—exceeded only by the cost of a house. (Some colleges cost *more* for four years than the average cost of a house in some states.)

College is more than a preparation for a career. Often the person who graduates has become a different person from what he or she was as an entering freshman. Moreover, the imprint of a particular college or university can remain for life. Decades later, people may say knowingly, "He was a West Pointer," or "She went to Bennington," or "He is a Chicago economist." Many writers have commented on the fact that Lyndon Johnson's relations with the Kennedys were soured by his awareness that they went to Harvard while he graduated from Southwest Texas State Teachers College. For better or worse, the choice of a college has lifelong implications.

✔ DIFFERENCES IN COLLEGES

At its best, the right college can open up whole vistas to the mind and be an exhilarating experience, like being born again. Many alumni are grateful for life for what their colleges did for them—and this gratitude translates into billions of dollars in donations annually to provide scholarships and other expenditures necessary to keep these opportunities alive for a new generation.

At its worst, college can be a tiresome chore without meaning—a burden that many cannot endure for four long years. It is not uncommon for a fourth or a half of all students on many campuses to fail to make it through to graduation. That is by no means the worst of it. Psychiatric problems are widespread at some of the most prestigious colleges, sometimes ending in suicide. At Harvard, a thousand students a year seek psychiatric help at the university's Mental Health Service.

When I taught at Cornell University during the 1960s, I was told that they averaged about a suicide a year among the students. Some years later, while teaching at U.C.L.A., I was surprised on my way to the office one morning to see an attractive, well-dressed young lady lying gracefully in the bushes, apparently asleep. Only the presence of policemen nearby alerted me to the grim reality: Less than an hour before, she had jumped from the roof of the building to her death. Somewhere, no doubt, there were parents whose hearts would be broken before nightfall.

In short, the stakes are very high, personally as well as educationally, when choosing a college. The problem is not to find a "good" college or the "best" college. The perfect college for one student can be a disaster for another. A student who would love Reed College would probably be miserable at Brigham Young University, and vice versa (among numerous differences, it is easier to get cocaine at Reed College than it is to get Coca-Cola at B.Y.U. Every significant feature of a college can differ enormously from one institution to another.

Academically, the quality of work that would get you an *A* at one college would not be good enough to get you a *C* at another. The average mathematics score on the Scholastic Aptitude Test among students at Harvey Mudd College is greater than the combined math and verbal S.A.T. scores at Cheyney University.

Socially, there are many places like Williams College, Mills College, or the Florida Institute of Technology, where men can spend the night in women's rooms. It is called "24-hour intervisitation" or "intervisitation unlimited," in the jargon with which academics surround plain facts. As one academic administrator at a west coast institution told me privately: "We don't know what goes on in the dormitories and we don't want to know." At the other end of the spectrum, Pepperdine University continues to maintain the kind of strict control over visits by the opposite sex that was widespread a generation ago.

At some colleges, you will see graffiti everywhere. At other colleges, you will see graffiti nowhere—not even in the toilets. Tuition alone costs over $10,000 a year at some colleges, but it is only $300 a year at Cooper Union—a good institution with an outstanding engineering school. Some colleges, such as Bard or Evergreen, are politically left and far left while others, such as Hillsdale or Wabash, are solidly conservative. Whenever people tell you what "everybody" is doing at colleges these days, they are wrong. There are some important general trends—positive and negative—but there is still an enormous range of diversity. This is both a challenge and an opportunity. Somewhere, there is at least one place that is good for each individual— and one is enough, but finding it will take some work. There are literally thousands of colleges and universities in the United States, some two-year, some four-year, some with only a few hundred students and others with more than 40,000; some in rural New England or overlooking Malibu Beach, and others in downtown New York, Atlanta, or Chicago.

✔ SOURCES OF ADVICE

There are a number of sources of help in sorting through all this, but you also need to keep a skeptical eye on some of those who are helping you. Alumni tend to have an ex- aggerated notion of how high their Alma Mater rates. Some will look you straight in the eye and tell you that Podunk A&M is just as good as any school in the Ivy League. Some even believe it. High school counselors can sometimes be helpful but they can also lead you straight into a catas- trophe. The quality of high school counselors varies as widely as the colleges themselves.

Some counselors present a special problem when they see their role as sidetracking the parents, so that the stu- dent can make his or her own decision, under the guidance of the counselor. Parents should not let themselves be in- timidated by the counselor's "expertise." If the decision turns out to be wrong for their child—and wrong can in- clude anything from flunking out or getting pregnant to being caught up in the drug culture for life—the counselor will not lose one dime or one hour's sleep. Each parent knows better than anyone else what it will cost to see his or her child ruined.

It is fashionable nowadays for educational "professionals" to look down their noses at those parents who don't go along with the latest fads, as if such parents were bumpkins or Archie Bunkers. But, when you think about it, the negative opinion of shallow people is a very small price to pay to safeguard your child's future. When my daughter's high school counselor wrote me that I would be "kept informed" as to what they were deciding about colleges, I knew it was time to ignore that counselor and seek information elsewhere.

There are a number of informative guides on the market which can give you useful information about particular colleges. But, although college guides may not vary as widely as counselors' opinions, they can still vary considerably. For example, according to *Barron's Profiles of American Colleges*, admission to Whitman College is rated "Very Competitive +" but *The ARCO Guide: The Right College* rates Whitman's admissions standards as "Non-competitive." While the *Insider's Guide to the Colleges* lists the psychology department at Knox College as among that school's best departments, Edward Fiske's *Selective Guide to Colleges* suggests that psychology is among Knox's worst departments.

However statistical, official, or "scientific" some guides may look, they are still written by human beings. That means that none can be followed blindly and all require further efforts on your part to get more information. The best can only point you in the right general direction. You must investigate further on your own. (Chapters 8–12 of this book suggest how to go about it.)

✔ TESTS AND ADMISSIONS

The most important information of all is information about the particular student, and that cannot be found in any guide. The student's academic level and individual personality are crucial in deciding which kinds of colleges make sense for him or her, and which should be eliminated from consideration at the outset. This elimination process is essential because you cannot read hundreds of institutional descriptions in a huge college guide, much less send away for catalogues and brochures to investigate each one further.

Each student's scholastic ability should be tested, preferably before the senior year of high school, to get some idea of what kinds of colleges to be thinking about. More than a million high school seniors annually take the Scholastic Aptitude Test (S.A.T.), the most widely used college entrance examination, and more than three-quarters of a million high school seniors take the American College Testing Program (A.C.T.) examination, which serves the same purpose. These tests are by no means perfect and critics have stirred up a great deal of controversy about their imperfections, both real and imaginary. Yet nothing better has come along.

The test results can be enormously valuable when it comes time to select a dozen or so institutions worth serious investigation. The average verbal score on the Scholastic Aptitude Test has been around 430 points in recent years and the average math score around 470 points, for a total of about 900 points out of a possible 1600. There are many very good colleges whose students' average combined S.A.T. scores total about 1000 and are therefore within the academic range for most high school students who go on to college. Some of the top colleges and universities, however, have students whose combined S.A.T. totals are about 1400, so that schools like these (Yale, Stanford, Cal Tech, M.I.T.) are far too demanding for most students.

A college's average S.A.T. score is a useful rough indication of whether your scores put you in or out of the ball park as far as that school is concerned. If your math and verbal S.A.T.'s combined are 100 points below the college's average, that is not out of the ball park. But if they are 200 points below, you are probably pressing your luck.

Every college has its anecdotes about students with low scores who did wonderfully. There are also illiterates who became millionaires. But most people go with the percentages, instead of betting their future on a long shot. College is too serious a choice to let other people's anecdotes lead you into a bad gamble. But that doesn't mean that there is no leeway at all in schools you can reasonably apply to.

Colleges and universities themselves allow considerable leeway in admitting students and few have a rigid cutoff according to test scores. At Emory University, for example, the average combined S.A.T. score of the freshman class is 1200 but the range is from 1010 to 1580. At many colleges, your chances of acceptance vary with test scores and class rank, but you do have a chance over a very wide range—and no certainty, even with a top record, at the more selective institutions. Amherst College, for example, admitted 46 percent of those who applied for the class of 1991 with verbal S.A.T. scores of 750 and above, and 14 percent of those who applied with verbal S.A.T.'s in the 500s. Harvard says: "Most of our successful applicants have test scores ranging from 500 to 800 but high test scores are no guarantee of admissions and low scores do not necessarily mean exclusion." That is also true at many other places.

Where the admissions pressures are not as extreme, high scores and high class rank create a much higher probability of admissions, but the general principle remains the same — no guarantees that you will be in or out. Duke University accepted 63 percent of those who scored 750 or higher on the verbal S.A.T., Bowdoin College 86 percent, and Davidson College 81 percent. In all three, less than half of those scoring in the 500s on verbal S.A.T. were admitted. Still, in absolute numbers, all three institutions accepted more students in the 500 range than in the 750 and up range. Such patterns are common in a variety of institutions and are found whether you look at verbal S.A.T., math S.A.T., class rank, A.C.T. score, or other indicators.

Colleges tend to take many things into account beside test scores, grade point averages, or class rankings. Some seek social diversity in their students and may accept lower test scores and other credentials from students whose ethnic group is statistically "under-represented." Some schools seek geographic diversity and may admit students from far away with somewhat lower qualifications than they demand from students located within their state or region. Others — especially state colleges and universities — do just the reverse and give preference to those within the state, both in admission standards and tuition charges.

Beyond some point, all this flexibility in admissions standards can be a trap for the student. Colleges serve their own institutional purposes by lowering standards for athletes, ethnic minorities, alumni children, and others, but the students admitted under these lower standards can find themselves in big trouble academically. The cold fact is that test scores and high school grades are correlated with college performance. Freshmen whose past performance falls well below those of their college classmates have less chance of surviving. All the pretty talk in the world about "diversity," or about how we are "not competing," does not change that.

Almost all colleges and universities will accept athletes with lower qualifications than other students—sometimes disgracefully lower. It is common at colleges and universities across the country for athletes to finish four years of school with no degree—not even in the easy subjects that many college athletes major in. It is considered very unusual that athletes at Penn State University generally graduate and that coach Joe Paterno, who insists that his players get an education, still manages to win football games "with real students," as *USA Today* put it.

Test scores are of course not the only indicator of academic ability. How well you did in high school is probably an even better guide to how well you will do in college. Unfortunately, grading standards vary so much from school to school—especially from a public school in the slums to a private boarding school in the suburbs—that it is more difficult to get a reliable measure of high school performance. Standardized admissions tests like the S.A.T and the A.C.T. came into general use precisely for this reason.

Academic standards in general, and test scores in particular, are a good way to begin eliminating some of the thousands of colleges and universities that are available, to get down to those worth serious investigation because they are within your academic range. (Virtually all college guides give the average test scores of various colleges.) Other considerations will reduce the number of colleges still further, until finally you have a short enough list to proceed with a closer look at specific schools, including perhaps a visit to the campuses.

✔ PERSONAL FACTORS

The personality, hopes, and style of the individual student are as crucial as academic ability when trying to match the person with the college. A shy, introverted student can easily get lost for four years on a campus with 30,000 or 40,000 students, sitting in classes so big that the professor knows no one's name and never calls on anyone for give-and-take discussion. The social life of such a person can be virtually non-existent in such a setting or—worse yet—may involve going along with whatever is being done by the group he or she falls in with, out of fear of loneliness. On the other hand, brash self-starters who know exactly what they want, and insist on getting it, may do all right in this setting—despite the anonymity, indifferent faculty members, and a large, suffocating bureaucracy. Most people are not at these extremes, but it makes an enormous difference where you stand on the spectrum. A small college, with perhaps a thousand or so students, is a much better bet for those who could easily get lost in a crowd or be overwhelmed by a massive bureaucracy to whom they are just a number.

Values and behavior patterns are also important in matching student and college. Not every 18-year-old girl is ready to live in a room with boys' rooms on each side of her, and not every parent thinks it's a good idea. At some colleges, one of the painful situations a girl can experience is having her roommate's boyfriend spend the night in their room.

Co-ed dorms are a fact of life on most campuses, but how people behave in them differs. Whether they are set up with different floors for men and women or in some other way may also affect that behavior. The attitudes of the other students and of college officials probably matter even more. Despite the popularity of co-ed dorms, some colleges still offer a choice of single-sex or co-ed dorms, and others still stick exclusively to single-sex dorms. If this is an important concern, then it should be added to the list of considerations used to select or eliminate colleges. Given the widespread acceptance of co-ed dorms, this consideration may narrow your list faster than some others. Still, you are looking for only about a half a dozen colleges to apply to and only one to attend. (There are many colleges where most students do *not* live in co-ed dorms, and a list of 50 of them can be found in Chapter 6.)

Religion is another aspect of values for many people. Some are simply looking for a campus where the religious person finds acceptance rather than condescension or sneers. Others want a college with a positive affirmation of religious values, or perhaps the values of their own particular faith or denomination. Almost all colleges and universities have houses of worship on campus, but they vary in how much they have beyond that. In general, the more stringent your requirements, the narrower your choices. Still, in purely quantitative terms, there are nearly a hundred Baptist colleges, more than a hundred Methodist colleges, and more than two hundred Catholic colleges. Lutherans, Mormons, Presbyterians, Quakers, and others also have their own institutions.

State colleges and universities are of course non-denominational and many of the top private institutions likewise have no special religious character, even when founded by, or nominally affiliated with, a particular church. Brandeis University is Jewish in origin but has large Christian chapels on campus and imposes no religious requirements on anyone. Catholic colleges and universities span a wide range of religious policies, as well as academic quality, with prestigious Georgetown University and high-quality Holy Cross College being among the best academically. Some of the more fundamentalist Protestant denominations have nothing comparable in academic standing to Georgetown or Holy Cross. The Quakers, however, established three of the top-rated colleges in the country in Swarthmore, Haverford, and Bryn Mawr, but here again the church connection imposes no special religious requirements on their students.

Where the religious affiliation does have an important effect on the campus environment, those whose own personal commitments match those of the institution may feel more at home—and those who don't share that commitment may feel more uncomfortable, or even isolated. Nearly 300 colleges have compulsory chapel attendance, for example. Other church-related colleges leave such matters entirely to the individual. But, even where the institution imposes no special rules, the fact that the student body is overwhelmingly of one faith can affect the whole atmosphere for those who share that faith, and for those who don't.

Some students (or their parents) are looking for colleges with structure, rules, and values. They want the faculty and the administration to establish a curriculum with required basic courses, as well as rules of conduct to guide the students' maturation from adolescent to adult. Other students and parents want freedom above all—freedom to take whatever courses arouse the greatest interest and freedom to live whatever lifestyle seems the most fulfilling. There are many colleges catering to both extremes, as well as others in the middle. Brooke Shields, for example, was able to graduate from Princeton without taking a single course in mathematics, history, chemistry, economics, physics, or biology. Some will think that was wonderful; others, that it was terrible. The important thing is for students and parents to think through what they want in this regard, and make that another point on which to select or eliminate colleges.

✔ PAYING FOR COLLEGE

Financial Aid

One thing that should not automatically eliminate any college is the cost of tuition. Despite the most modest income, or even poverty, it may be possible to attend the most expensive college or university. The top colleges and universities are often the most richly endowed, and can afford to offer the largest amount of financial aid. Harvard, for example, provides financial aid to two-thirds of its students. There were more than 600 scholarships awarded in the Harvard Class of 1990, averaging well over $6,000 a year each. In addition, there are also loans available from the college itself and from the government, totalling more than $7 million a year. As a low-income student myself more than 30 years ago, I went to Harvard because there was simply no place else that I could afford to go full-time.

While not all institutions can match the massive financial aid available at Harvard, many less well-known institutions are able to do quite well in this respect. The Rochester Institute of Technology, Whitworth College, and Willamette University, for example, each averages $5,500 per student annually in financial aid based on need—and each has tuition about half that of Harvard's, so the money goes further. At many state universities, the tuition for state residents is quite low, so that a fairly modest financial aid package will be sufficient for even a poverty-stricken student. At the University of California at Berkeley, for example, 40 percent of the students receive financial aid based on need, and while such aid averages only $3,500 per year, the tuition at Berkeley (for California residents) is only about one-tenth the tuition at Harvard.

At least partial financial aid is widely available, even to students from families whose annual income exceeds $50,000. At many colleges only a small minority of students actually pay the full tuition listed in the catalogue. The larger the tuition, the more likely that is to be so. You certainly don't need to be either poverty-stricken or a genius to get financial aid of some kind. More than 900 colleges, universities, and technical institutes provide financial aid for *every* freshman who demonstrates any "need" by their criteria.

While most financial aid in recent years has been based on "need" as that is broadly defined by the college, a few institutions are beginning to move back toward scholarships based on scholarship, though still retaining need-based financial aid as well. Among the institutions where non-need-based financial aid averages $5,000 a year or more per recipient are the University of Chicago, Boston University, Tulane, Holy Cross, Northwestern, Mills College, Villanova, Trinity College (Connecticut), and the Polytechnic Institute of New York. Moreover, state universities usually have low enough tuition that smaller scholarships than this will be more than adequate.

Despite all this, it will still require some effort for an average student from an average-income family to finance a good college education. Perhaps the best place to start looking for specific colleges to match both the academic and financial capabilities of such a student would be Edward

Fiske's guide, *The Best Buys in College Education.* Unfortunately, like most college guides, it does not include two-year colleges, which are another option when income and academic records are both limited.

The local reputation of two-year colleges is about all that you can go by, in many cases. It may be worth asking in the admissions office of a reputable state university how easy it is to transfer in from the two-year college you are considering, and how well previous transfer students from there have survived in the more rigorous state university. Even if you don't plan to transfer to that state university, the information can be valuable when choosing among two-year colleges. Some states have formal policies requiring the admission of community college graduates to the state university system. However, that tells you nothing about how many community college graduates do go on, or with what results. But there is a useful list of more than a hundred two-year colleges where more than three-quarters of their graduates go on to four-year colleges in *National College Databank,* published by Peterson's Guides, Inc.

College Jobs

Whatever the student's academic ability and financial needs, it is usually best to avoid working at a job while going to school, or to minimize the hours if it is unavoidable. A bigger loan is far preferable to more hours of work. College represents an enormous investment of time, money, effort, and emotion. This investment should not be jeopardized for the relatively small sums of money to be earned on a part-time job.

The hours spent on the job are not a real measure of how much it takes away from learning. It is not just the hours, but the fact that these hours are usually fixed, which reduces the effectiveness of study. Some subjects—especially math and the sciences—require sustained, concentrated study for as long as it takes to wrestle with a given problem. If you are two hours into your assignment when time comes to go off to your job, there is no assurance that you can come back three or four hours later and pick it up right where you left off. The mind just doesn't work that way. Moreover, the fatigue factor affects your sharpness, whether you go to work before or in the middle of your studying. You may not feel tired, but losing a little of your edge can be the difference between understanding and not understanding a difficult subject. It would be truly penny-wise and pound-foolish to find yourself gradually forced out of difficult—and rewarding—subjects into something easier, simply because a part-time job left you operating at less than 100 percent.

Because your earning power will almost always be greater after graduating, it will take fewer hours of work to repay a college loan then than it would take to earn the same money while in college. Moreover, the time you spend working after graduation does not hurt your education and the academic record you take to a graduate school or an employer. From every perspective, it makes sense to borrow more money rather than spend more hours on a job while in college. College loans usually are not difficult to repay and are not due until your education is completed, even if that is after graduate school.

No one wants to begin a career carrying a burden of debt. But a good academic record is usually worth dollars and cents, whether in terms of starting salary, or in terms of how long it takes to land a good job, or your chances for a graduate fellowship. Even in the first few years after finishing college or graduate school, this can more than offset your payments on a college loan. In the long run, getting the best preparation for a rewarding career and life means far more than the money you earn on a campus job.

✔ EXPECTATIONS

People differ not only in their academic abilities, personalities, finances, and values, but also in what they expect from a college. To some, a college means ivy-covered buildings, fraternities, sororities, football, and parties, with academic work almost an afterthought. They will probably have no trouble finding colleges to accommodate them. To others, colleges are places to prepare for a well-paying career, either immediately after graduation or after medical school, law school, or the like. These individuals will have to exercise care in selecting their colleges, for their academic backgrounds can have much to do with their later success in their careers. Finally, there are those for whom college is primarily a place to develop their minds and discover new dimensions of life. These will probably have the hardest task of all in selecting the right institution—and perhaps the most fulfilling rewards when they find it. Scholar and best-selling author Allan Bloom recalled how, as a youngster, "I saw the University of Chicago for the first time and somehow sensed that I had discovered my life." That discovery can take place in many places and in many ways for many people.

Whatever you are seeking in a college, and whatever abilities you bring to it, what is crucial is that you understand what your requirements and capabilities are. There are simply too many colleges, universities, and institutes of technology for intelligent selections to be made without first understanding clearly your own goals and your resources for meeting them. The basic theme of this chapter has been "Know thyself." The theme of the chapters that follow is "Know thy college."

CHAPTER 2

UNIVERSITIES

In a country with thousands of institutions of higher education, with widely varying standards and atmospheres, one of the ways of trying to bring some order out of this overwhelming complexity is to first break them down into a few general categories. Most of these institutions are universities, liberal arts colleges, or institutes of technology (engineering schools). Each type has its own special advantages and disadvantages.

Whatever kind of institution you are considering, one of the more mundane, but potentially important, problems to be aware of is confusing the names of institutions. Obviously, what you learn about one place may not be at all true of another place with the same or similar name. There are, for example, four independent institutions named Trinity College, located in four different states—not counting Trinity College at Duke University, Trinity Christian College, or Trinity University. There are also two separate institutions named Wheaton College, two named Judson College, and three named Columbia College, not counting the one at Columbia University. In addition, Miami University in Ohio is often confused with the University of Miami in Florida, just as Washington University in St. Louis can be confused with the University of Washington in Seattle or George Washington University in the District of Columbia. A name like Indiana University of Pennsylvania invites multiple confusions, since there is an Indiana University in Bloomington and a University of Pennsylvania in Philadelphia.

Many state university systems have campuses in different cities with very different standards and purposes, but all using the same name. The University of California at Santa Cruz is not like the University of California at Davis—as both will tell you. U.C. Santa Cruz is an experimental institution with a Bohemian flavor, while U.C. Davis tends to be pre-professional in academic orientation and to attract a very different student body, geared to such concerns. The University of South Florida in Tampa is a typical large state university (about 28,000 students) but, in Sarasota, New College of the University of South Florida has less than 500 students, with combined SAT scores averaging more than 200 points higher and an impressive record of sending a higher proportion of its students on to get Ph.D.'s than most Ivy League schools do.

Whether talking, reading, or writing for information, be sure to know the exact name (and location) of the college you are considering. You don't want either positive or negative information about one place to influence your decision about another.

✔ TEACHING VERSUS RESEARCH

Universities are likely to be the best known educational institutions, whether because of their football teams (Ohio State, Notre Dame, Alabama), their basketball teams (U.C.L.A., Georgetown), or their scholarship and research (Harvard, Chicago, Berkeley). None is famous for its undergraduate teaching, though a few may in fact deserve to be. Undergraduate teaching is simply not as newsworthy as a Rose Bowl victory or a Nobel Prize. There is less relationship between institutional renown and undergraduate education in a university than in any other kind of educational institution. Nowhere is it more necessary to avoid being dazzled by big names.

Parents and students need to understand—as clearly and as early as possible—that while their top priority may be a good education, that is not necessarily the top priority of university professors. The more prestigious the university, the less likely is the teaching of undergraduates to be paramount. For example, *Time* magazine summarized criticisms of top Harvard professors as "too engaged in their own research, too busy with outside consulting or just too lordly to bother with anything so trivial as an undergraduate." One renowned Harvard professor of government was described as talking to a class of 15 students while gazing over their heads, "as if addressing the House of Lords." Much the same picture emerges repeatedly in the *Confidential Guide* published by Harvard students, where another professor of government was described as "completely disorganized" in his lectures and "inept at managing classroom discussions." Words like "disorganized" and "rambling" appear again and again in descriptions of the lectures of particular Harvard professors in fields as disparate as music, anthropology, and women's studies. In a course on genetics, both the professor and his teaching assistants are described as "often inadequately prepared" and in an introductory chemistry course, "lectures have bordered on the incomprehensible."

These problems are not peculiar to Harvard. Princeton's *Student Course Guide* likewise repeatedly characterizes lectures as "rambling," "confusing," "unorganized," or even "incoherent," whether the subject is architecture, biology, mathematics, chemistry, economics, Afro-American studies, mechanical and aerospace engineering, or Near-Eastern studies. Lectures were especially confusing in an economics course in which the professor "got lost in his own equations." In an electrical engineering course, the lecturer "literally read the book aloud in his lecture." In one math course, the "lectures were spotty, poorly organized, and poorly presented." In another, mathematical proofs were simply "begun and never finished."

None of these things is peculiar to Harvard or Princeton. The point here is that *world-class universities do not mean world-class teaching*. At both these institutions (and others) there are also some professors who are highly praised by the students for superb teaching. The terms in which these teachers are praised by the students are often revealing: "A research star who actually considers teaching worthwhile," "one of the few professors who answers his own telephone," "everything that Harvard is supposed to be, but usually isn't."

At Harvard, Princeton, and other institutions, the characterization appearing again and again in discussions of lectures by highly praised professors is "well-organized." Anyone who has taught difficult material knows that producing a clear and well-structured lecture can take hours of preparation, even for someone who has taught the subject before. World-class scholars, vying for international pre-eminence in their fields, often have neither the time, the teaching talent, nor the inclination to produce the kinds of lectures that make a subject clear and alive for undergraduates.

Important as lectures are, opportunities for interaction with professors outside the classroom—in their offices or at informal gatherings—can also be an important part of an educational experience. However, according to a distinguished accreditation panel visiting Harvard in 1987, "only the most aggressive and persistent undergraduate" is likely to have any "faculty-student interaction outside of the classroom" with senior Harvard professors. Harvard is by no means unique in this respect, nor are junior faculty members or even teaching assistants always accessible at research universities.

The junior faculty and the graduate students who serve as teaching assistants at many universities have other distractions and pressures that keep them from investing great amounts of time in teaching. Their whole future and that of their families hang in the balance while they try to complete their research, so as to establish themselves in their professions. Many graduate students never get the Ph.D. degree for which they have sacrificed years of their lives. Most junior faculty members at leading research universities are let go after a few years, except for those rare individuals whose research output marks them as stars to be given tenure. In short, junior as well as senior faculty at many universities have strong incentives to give teaching a low priority. The very process by which a top university maintains its prestige and visibility in the world can undermine the education of undergraduates.

The teaching role of graduate students at universities is far larger than many people—especially parents and high school students—realize. Harvard has about 400 people teaching who are not faculty members but teaching assistants, teaching fellows, and the like—usually graduate students, understandably preoccupied with completing their own education. Even when called "teaching assistants," they do much more than simply assist professors with grading exams or preparing science labs. Most of the classes in introductory calculus at Harvard are taught by teaching assistants. Many teaching assistants are foreign, and a recurring complaint in the Harvard students' *Confidential Guide* is that their English is often hard to understand. As for the advisory role of these non-faculty teachers, according to the *Harvard Salient* (a student newspaper), "academic advising can be a sad joke, often consisting of nothing more than a harried tutor's cursory glance at the study card. Many of us qualify as 'phantom students' who go through Harvard without ever meeting a full professor."

The great state universities have similar problems, often to an even greater extent than Harvard and other large private universities. The University of California at Berkeley is unsurpassed as a research institution, its faculty have received many Nobel Prizes, its graduate programs rank above those of Harvard in several fields, and Berkeley is often rated number one among the nation's universities. However, none of this translates into an outstanding undergraduate education. At Berkeley, there are estimated to be more than twice as many graduate students teaching as at Harvard. In addition, Berkeley has large numbers of part-time junior faculty, who support themselves by having other jobs—and therefore other demands on their time besides teaching. Finally, the huge size of the university—more than 30,000 students—ensures that undergraduate education is impersonal, bureaucratic, and sometimes chaotic.

Many of the other outstanding state universities show a similar pattern. The universities of Michigan, Wisconsin, Minnesota, Illinois, and U.C.L.A. are all among the top 10 in a number of fields of graduate study and are usually included in lists of the country's leading universities. However, neither they nor Berkeley is even among the top 70 when it comes to the percentage of their own undergraduates who go on through graduate school to receive a Ph.D. Many small colleges are far more successful in this respect. These include not only such well-known colleges as Reed, Swarthmore, Oberlin, and Amherst, but also such little-known colleges as Wabash, Davidson, Occidental, and Birmingham-Southern.

There is nothing necessarily immoral about the priorities of a research university. But parents and students need to understand what they are getting into when choosing a famous university, whether in the Ivy League or the flagship of their state university system. Some universities try to balance the pressures for research results with pressures to provide good undergraduate teaching as well, though that is much easier said than done. More important, some conscientious professors are genuinely concerned about college students, and such professors can be found at all academic levels and in all kinds of institutions—whether universities, liberal arts colleges, or technical institutes. At the University of California at San Diego, as at Harvard and Princeton, there are professors who draw praise from a student newspaper (*The California Review* in this case) as "a great teacher . . . tolerant of opposing viewpoints and respectful of his students." But while you can find such teachers everywhere, you cannot find them in the same proportions everywhere, and at some universities they are quite rare.

Those professors who enjoy teaching more than research are likely to seek out the small liberal arts college— or have to go there after being forced out of research universities for not publishing enough. Winning the "teacher of the year" award at a research university will carry very little weight when time comes to have one's contract renewed or to be voted on for tenure. In 1987, a Harvard professor whose credentials included such an award was notified that his contract would not be renewed. I personally know three other professors at three different institutions who were notified that their contracts would not be renewed after they had won "teacher of the year" awards. One referred to the award as "travel money."

The issue of teaching versus research has been debated innumerable times and is unlikely to be settled any time soon. What is important to someone seeking good teaching is to find out where it is most likely to be found. At a top research university, where the professor knows that "publish or perish" are his career choices, it is unrealistic to expect that most will make teaching their top priority. To some, teaching is purely incidental.

✔ SIZE

Large Universities
Universities have great advantages as well as disadvantages—and whether one outweighs the other depends entirely on what kind of person you are. If you are the kind

of person who can find your way through the maze with little or no help, who can separate the wheat from the chaff when selecting courses, and is a self-starter when it comes to studying, doing assignments, or making friends, you may be ready to tackle the largest, most impersonal university and be able to benefit from the best that it has to offer. You should be aware, however, of just how large many universities are. There are 20,000 or more students on each of about a hundred or more campuses across the country, including more than 40,000 on the following campuses, each the main campus of a state university:

University of Minnesota	62,266 students
Ohio State University	53,446 students
University of Texas	47,973 students
University of Wisconsin	44,218 students
Michigan State University	42,193 students
Arizona State University	40,538 students

Each of the above represents the number of students on one campus, not counting students at other campuses of the state university system. These figures do, however, include undergraduates, graduate students, and students in professional schools on campus, such as medical schools and law schools. But each of the six campuses above (and others) has more than 30,000 undergraduates alone, with nearly 50,000 undergraduates being on the main campus of the University of Minnesota. While these half dozen universities are the largest, there are many more that are sufficiently large to be impersonal and bureaucratic. There are 10,000 or more undergraduates alone on well over 200 campuses in the United States.

Often the problems created by size are made worse when many students do not live on campus, but are scat-

tered across a large area—a few living in dormitories, some
living in rooming houses, some sharing apartments, some
commuting from miles away. At an institution like this,
there simply is no college community, and an individual can
easily get lost completely, with no one knowing that he or
she exists, except as a name and a number on computer
printouts. Both the academic and the psychic consequences
of this isolation can be devastating.

Discussions among students can be a major part of an
undergraduate education on campuses where there is
enough of a college community for such discussions to take
place regularly. At some colleges, students are encouraged
to work together on difficult problem sets that can take
hours to figure out, even with everyone in a group pitching
in. In some math, science, and engineering courses, these
problem sets not only test your understanding but are an
essential tool in getting you beyond the generalities of the
textbook or the lecture to a penetrating understanding of
the real complexities involved. Students not only discuss
the material from their courses, clarifying their own
thoughts in the process; they also keep each other abreast
of all sorts of opportunities, dangers, and deadlines on campus. Students are also a valuable source of counseling on
what courses to take and what professors to seek out (or
to avoid). All these academic benefits of student interaction
are lost at a commuter school with no real college community. The personal losses, as far as morale and social development are concerned, may be even greater.

Statistics on the percentage of students living on campus can give you a clue about all this, but are not always
the last word. Both at the University of California at Davis
and at U.C.L.A., about 70 percent of the students live off
campus. But the little college town of Davis is not sprawling

Los Angeles, which covers an area 50 percent larger than the five boroughs of New York combined. Moreover, the neighborhood in the immediate vicinity of U.C.L.A. is too high-rent for most students to be able to live there. The net result is that U.C.L.A. students are scattered far and wide (one of my students lived 50 miles away) while U.C. Davis students live sufficiently clustered around the university to preserve something of a college community. This is one of the things to ask about during a campus visit: Where do the students live?

Although big universities are not usually places to look for individual attention, they do have other beneficial features. One of the advantages of many universities is the vast range of subjects covered and the vast range of courses under each subject. At U.C. Davis, a fairly modest-sized institution (20,000 students) as state universities go, there are 48 subjects in which to major in the undergraduate College of Letters and Sciences alone, compared to 25 at Hillsdale College, 21 at Bates College, and 20 at Beloit College, all fairly typical of liberal arts colleges in this regard. Within a given department, the disparities tend to be even greater. At U.C. Davis' College of Letters and Sciences, there are more than 50 undergraduate courses in mathematics, compared to less than half that many at Hillsdale, Bates, or Beloit.

Precise numbers are not crucial, because some schools are on quarter systems and others on semesters or trimesters, and some courses are offered every year while others are offered less frequently. Nevertheless, when disparities reach certain magnitudes, the general picture is clear: Big universities offer a greater variety of subjects and more courses within each subject. The chances of finding that special subject that will really ignite your interest, and of being able to pursue it further, are greater at a large university. Not only are there usually more courses available in the undergraduate liberal arts college of a university than in an independent liberal arts college, many universities like U.C. Davis also have undergraduate colleges of engineering, agricultural science, and other subjects, where you may enroll in particular courses that interest you. Moreover, there are also graduate courses available in case you want to pursue your interest in a particular subject further after exhausting the undergraduate courses that deal with it.

In addition to offering a wider range of intellectual resources, large universities often offer a wider range of physical resources as well—computers, library facilities, and science laboratories, for example. However, it is necessary to assess these resources in comparison to the number of people who will be using them. The University of California at Davis has about seven times as many books in its library as Beloit College has, but there are nearly 18 times as many students at U.C. Davis.

Even the question as to what courses are available depends on the number of people. While a large university may have far more courses listed in its catalogue, more of these courses may be closed when they reach their enrollment limit (usually based on the size of the classroom). So, while it *may* be possible to sample a wider variety of courses at a big university, it may also be more difficult to take the basic courses in the right sequence because the classes fill up and are then closed to further enrollment. During one academic year, for example, Berkeley students were refused permission to enroll in a chosen course more than 15,000 times. That's only about once per undergraduate per year. But, depending upon what the courses are, not being allowed to enroll in courses you want four times during your college career can throw a monkey wrench into your whole program and set back your graduation.

The larger universities tend to predominate in many academic fields, though some smaller ones make a strong showing as well. When faculty members across the country ranked the top 10 graduate departments in their respective fields, the following institutions had departments among the top 10 the most times:

		No. of Top 10 Depts.
1.	University of California at Berkeley	28
2.	Stanford University	25
3.	Harvard University	22
4.	University of California at Los Angeles (U.C.L.A.)	18
5.*	University of Chicago	17
5.*	Princeton University	17
7.	Yale University	16
8.*	University of Michigan	15
8.*	Massachusetts Institute of Technology	15
10.*	Columbia University	14
10.*	University of Wisconsin	14

*Tied in ranking.
Source: Conference Board of Associated Research Councils

Like most other lists, this list contains both useful information and pitfalls. One pitfall in this case is that universities differ so much in size that they also differ in the number of departments they have. Not all are big enough to have departments in fields that attract a relatively small percentage of their students. Thus, while the University of Minnesota is number one in geography, Rice and Princeton have no geography departments at all, and so could not possibly be among the top 10 in that field. Huge institutions like Berkeley, Wisconsin, or U.C.L.A. have at least a chance of being in the top 10 in virtually every field, while Chicago, Princeton, or Johns Hopkins do not. This does not make the rankings meaningless, because many other huge universities seldom or never make the top 10 list in any field. On the other hand, some universities not on this select list were nevertheless among the top 10 departments in some fields—the University of Illinois in a number of mathematical, scientific, and engineering fields, as well as in music, linguistics, history, and political science, for example. In addition to the University of Illinois, some other very large universities that show up among the top 10 in a number of fields include Penn, Minnesota, Texas, Washington (Seattle), Purdue, and Cornell.

While rankings of graduate departments may in many cases have very limited relevance to undergraduate education, they do indicate something about the presence of world-class professors on campus. Further investigation can determine how many actually teach undergraduate courses and how effectively. For those students who are able to thrive in a large university setting, it can be a special opportunity to study under one of the leading scholars in a field, either in an undergraduate course or perhaps in a graduate course by the senior year. Similar opportunities may be even more available in some of the smaller universities, where teaching may receive more attention.

Smaller Universities

Not all universities are huge—not even all the world-class research universities. The University of Chicago, which must be included on any list of the great universities of the world, has less than 9,000 students—including those in its medical school, law school, and other graduate and professional programs. Princeton has less than 7,000 total students at all levels, and Johns Hopkins less than 4,000 graduates and undergraduates on its main campus. There are also many less renowned universities of similar sizes. These smaller universities may escape some of the worst bureaucratic excesses of the huge, impersonal institutions, and graduate teaching assistants may play a much smaller role in their undergraduate programs, but "publish or perish" remains the watchword of the faculty at the most prestigious of these universities and at those that aspire to that status. Nevertheless, smaller size seems to pay educational dividends to the undergraduates.

Universities whose undergraduate colleges are small are disproportionately represented among those whose graduates continue on to receive the Ph.D. The University of Chicago, whose undergraduate college has only about 3,000 students, has had nearly one-fourth of its bachelor's degree recipients continue on to receive doctorates over the past 30 years—putting it first among all universities in that respect—compared to 16 percent at Harvard. Rice, Brandeis, Wesleyan, Princeton, Johns Hopkins, and the University of Rochester also have relatively small numbers of undergraduates and they rank well ahead of Berkeley, Michigan, Penn, U.C.L.A., and many other large, highly regarded universities in the proportion of their undergraduates who later achieve the Ph.D., though in absolute numbers the bigger schools are ahead.

The significance of these data on later doctoral degrees reaches well beyond those people who plan to go on to graduate school. It says something about the quality and effectiveness of undergraduate teaching in general when significant percentages of the alumni are able to continue on to the doctorate. It says something about the importance of size that so many of the top institutions in this respect are small—small universities as well as small liberal arts colleges and small engineering schools. Not one institution among the top 70 has 12,000 undergraduates on campus. Most have less than half that number. Many of the leading universities that grant Ph.D.'s have far larger student bodies, and it is remarkable that their own undergraduates are not as successful at continuing on to that level as the undergraduates from smaller schools, many of which do not even have graduate programs of their own.

Not all smaller colleges and universities are private. There are a few smaller state-supported institutions worth noting, especially if the high tuition charged by private institutions is a problem. The University of California at Riverside has less than 4,000 undergraduates and houses most of them on campus, unlike Berkeley, U.C.L.A., and the rest of the U.C. system. Douglass College in New Jersey is about the same size and has a lovely campus (which I remember fondly as my first teaching post). Virginia has two state-supported liberal arts colleges: Mary Washington College (about 2,300 students) and William and Mary College (about 3,200 full-time undergraduates), in addition to the large and highly regarded University of Virginia. Evergreen State College in Olympia, Washington, has less than 3,000 students. The Morris campus of the University of Minnesota has less than 2,000 students. St. Mary's College, a state-supported institution in Maryland, has about 1,200 students. Florida's New College has less than 500 students, a good faculty, outstanding surroundings, and a successful experimental education program.

While some small-sized universities like Chicago pride themselves on successfully combining teaching and research, there are pressures even here to sacrifice the undergraduates for the sake of the graduate program. For example, there are grumblings from both students and faculty at the University of Chicago over the gradually increasing class size there and the increased use of teaching assistants. One professor refers to an "excruciating" problem of "steady pressure from graduate departments on the College to allow grad students to teach, as is the case at Harvard or Stanford." This will allow Chicago's graduate students to enter the competitive job market with teaching experience behind them and also allow the university to get its classes taught more cheaply than with professors—but all at a cost to the undergraduate. How far Chicago will move in the direction of Harvard, Stanford, and other large research universities in this regard is something to be checked out individually, as it may change from year to year.

Some smaller universities are essentially teaching institutions only. Depending on the proportions of graduate students and undergraduates, the smaller universities shade off into the category of liberal arts colleges. It is arbitrary to refer to institutions with only a relative handful of graduate students as "universities," when Bryn Mawr has hundreds of graduate students and even awards the Ph.D., while still being called a college. Lawrence University, Denison University, or Fisk University, for example, are more accurately described as colleges. There is nothing wrong with being a college rather than a university. What is important is to be aware of the real nature of an institution when making your choices.

CHAPTER 3

LIBERAL ARTS COLLEGES

Liberal arts colleges, like universities, come in almost unlimited varieties. Some small liberal arts colleges are part
of major universities. The undergraduate college at Johns
Hopkins and at Rice each has less than 3,000 students. On
the other hand, Brooklyn College alone has a larger enrollment of undergraduates than either of these universities
has total students enrolled at all levels. Huge colleges have
many of the same characteristics as huge universities. The
special characteristics of liberal arts colleges show up most
clearly in the smaller institutions.

✔ SIZE

The schools that epitomize the advantages and disadvantages of the liberal arts college are the independent
institutions with a thousand or two thousand students,
usually in a smaller town or a rural area. Here the student is less likely to be lost in a crowd on campus or

distracted by the bright lights of off-campus activities. Anyone who has seen Walla Walla, Washington (where Whitman College is located) or Aurora, New York (home of Wells College) is likely to conclude that any mischief a student gets into there will probably be on-campus mischief. Many of these schools are often referred to as "safe" because of their small town or rural locations. Where drugs abound, however, this may be a misplaced term, but often physical safety from others is not a major concern in such places.

The classic small liberal arts college is more than a pleasant place where other people know you, though that is not a small consideration for a student living away from home for the first time—especially a shy student. Academically, the learning process can be far more manageable where professors are teachers first and foremost. One of the best taught introductory economics classes I ever saw was taught by the late Ben Rogge at Wabash College in Indiana. Few students at Harvard would ever get such a good foundation in the subject. Ben, rest his soul, had obviously thought through all the pitfalls of the subject and led the student safely around them. A history professor at Hillsdale College had a similar knack of engaging students in what could easily be a dry and tedious subject—all the while casually sipping his morning coffee.

The importance of such teachers and the individual attention of a small college varies greatly with the student. For some students, such an environment is priceless and crucial to their social maturation as well as intellectual development. Some other students are going to master the subject and the situation no matter where they are. These latter students may derive no great advantages from going to a liberal arts college, so for them it may be a questionable trade-off to pass up the resources of a university or of a larger community, if that is what they want.

✔ COLLEGES VERSUS UNIVERSITIES

Liberal arts colleges are *not* watered-down universities. They often provide not only a more stimulating undergraduate education but also a more solid foundation for graduate school. We have already noted the irony that many large universities, with some of the top Ph.D. programs in the nation, have very unimpressive proportions of their own undergraduates go on to receive Ph.D.'s, compared to the proportions among students from small liberal arts colleges.

Being larger, universities of course generally have larger absolute numbers of their alumni go on to receive doctorates. But, size for size, the leading liberal arts colleges have no trouble holding their own with even the leading private universities. For example, among the institutions listed below, all with similar numbers of undergraduates and with composite S.A.T. scores of 1200 or more, the following numbers of their graduates went on to earn doctorates during the decade 1977–1986:

Oberlin College	998
Johns Hopkins University	658
Brandeis University	649
Rice University	618
Smith College	605
Wesleyan University	448
Colgate University	334
Holy Cross College	283

Source: National Research Council

No doubt there are many reasons for the variations within this select group, so exact numbers and exact rankings are not crucial. But the point here is simply that graduates of liberal arts colleges certainly hold their own with graduates of universities. Indeed, some even *smaller* liberal arts colleges have enough doctorates among their alumni to be comparable to the institutions in this group—for example, Mount Holyoke (447) and Swarthmore (535).

This particular list was selected to get similar-sized institutions with academically similar entering freshmen—which is not easy to do, since universities tend to be larger than colleges. An even better comparison would be among all colleges and universities, using *percentages* of students continuing on to the Ph.D., to allow for differences in their respective sizes. On this basis, the liberal arts colleges outdo the universities decisively when it comes to the proportion of their graduates who go on to complete the doctorate. For a 30-year period beginning in 1951, the following institutions had more than one-eighth of their graduates go on to receive the Ph.D.:

1. Harvey Mudd College
2. California Institute of Technology
3. Reed College
4. University of Chicago
5. Massachusetts Institute of Technology
6. Swarthmore College
7. Haverford College
8. Oberlin College
9. Harvard University
10. New College of the University of South Florida
11. University of California at San Diego

12.* Amherst College

12.* Carleton College

12.* Cooper Union for the Advancement of Science and Art

12.* Pomona College

16. Rice University

17. Brandeis University

18. Eckerd College

19. Wabash College

20. Bryn Mawr College

*Tied in ranking.

Source: Change magazine, Nov./Dec. 1986

Liberal arts colleges outnumber universities 10 to 6 among these 20 institutions, with the other 4 being engineering schools (Harvey Mudd, Cal Tech, M.I.T., Cooper Union). Such renowned universities as Yale, Stanford, and Princeton do not have as high a proportion of their alumni go on to receive Ph.D.'s as any of the colleges on this list.

There are many indications of the difference that size makes. Three of the top 10 institutions on the list have less than a thousand students each (Harvey Mudd, Cal Tech, New College). Among the universities on the list, most have small undergraduate colleges and none has as many as 20,000 total students on campus. Even within the same state university system, the University of California at San Diego has a higher percentage of students go on to doctorates than the larger and more prestigious Berkeley and U.C.L.A. campuses. So do U.C. Riverside, U.C. Irvine, and U.C. Santa Cruz. It is hard to see what advantage any of these campuses has over Berkeley and U.C.L.A., except that they are not as huge.

✔ FINDING SMALL COLLEGES

Because liberal arts colleges are not homogeneous, there is the same urgent need to match the individual to the institution that there is in the case of universities. But many fine liberal arts colleges are little known outside their home state or region. Someone living in California is more likely to have some idea how Duke University differs from the University of Alabama than to understand how Davidson College differs from Birmingham-Southern—though the latter schools are in the same two states as the former. By the same token, even a well-informed New Yorker may have no idea what the difference is between such west-coast colleges as Pitzer and Whitman, even when there is some awareness of how Stanford differs from Berkeley.

These difficulties in learning about small liberal arts colleges are reflected in the geographical origins of their students. Muhlenberg is a respectable college in Pennsylvania but 88 percent of its students come from just three states— New Jersey (38%), Pennsylvania (31%), and New York (19%). Only 2 percent are from outside the northeast quadrant. Similarly, 70 percent of Davidson College students come from the southeast, and Knox College receives 70 percent of its students from Illinois alone. It is an exceptional liberal arts college that can draw more than half its students from out of state, and even so, the bulk of the students usually come from adjoining states. This is no problem if the kind of school you want is in your area. But if the combination of things you are looking for reduces your choices drastically, the perfect place for you may be hundreds of miles away and wholly unknown to you when you begin your search.

What this all means is that choosing the right liberal

arts college can involve much more research than choosing
a university or institute of technology, if only because there
are more unknown gems to be discovered. You may never
have heard of Gustavus Adolphus College, but when more
than 60 percent of its alumni donate money annually, you
know that some people have lasting gratitude for what they
found there. You may never have heard of Davidson College, but it ranked above Amherst, Williams, Smith, and
Wellesley in the total number of doctorates in mathematics
received by its graduates over a decade—even though each
of these better-known colleges has more students than
Davidson.

College guides can be very helpful in the search for the
right liberal arts college, especially those guides that sketch
something of the flavor of each college, rather than simply
inundate you with statistics. *The Insiders Guide to the Colleges* and Edward Fiske's *Selective Guide to the Colleges*
can both be very useful and probably both should be read
to get at least two views of each institution. Fiske's *Best
Buys in Colleges* can also be useful, not just from a financial
angle, but also because it goes further down the academic
pecking order than the other two and turns up schools that
may be well worth considering, especially by students of
more modest academic achievement.

Most students go to college in their own state. This is
especially true of community college students (94%), less
true of four-year college students (77%), and still less so of
students attending top-level colleges and universities (less
than one-fifth of the students at Amherst or Harvard are
from Massachusetts). However, because geography is usually a factor in choosing a college, small liberal arts colleges
will be listed regionally here, so that those who would prefer to remain in the same general area of the country can

see what is available there before looking farther away. These colleges will also be grouped according to the general level of their S.A.T. scores so that you can begin your search among institutions whose students' academic capabilities are similar to your own. This obviously does not prevent your looking at institutions in more than one S.A.T. bracket. If your S.A.T. score is 1120, for example, this does not mean that you should disdain to consider a college whose median S.A.T. is 1080, or be afraid to think about going to a college whose median S.A.T. is an even 1200. But a composite S.A.T. difference of 200 points or more should make you think long and hard about the dangers of academic mismatching.

Liberal arts colleges with 3,000 students or less and combined S.A.T. scores averaging 1200 or above are shown below, listed alphabetically within each region. This list includes both independent colleges and those that belong to universities. Those colleges and universities with asterisks alongside their names have had more than 7 percent of their graduates go on to receive Ph.D.'s over a 30-year period.

Combined S.A.T. 1200 +

Northeast: Amherst*, Barnard*, Bowdoin*, Brandeis*, Bryn Mawr*, Colgate, Columbia*, Haverford*, Johns Hopkins*, Lafayette, Middlebury, St. John's* (Maryland), Smith, Swarthmore*, Trinity College (Connecticut), Union (New York), Vassar, Wellesley*, Wesleyan* (Connecticut), Williams*.

South: Davidson*, New College*, Rice*, Trinity University (Texas), University of Dallas, Washington & Lee, William & Mary.

West: Claremont McKenna, Pomona*, Reed*.

Midwest: Carleton*, Oberlin*, University of Chicago*.

While these are all top-level schools in terms of the average test scores of their entering freshmen, they vary enormously in the academic reputation of their faculties, the nature of their curricula, their approaches to teaching, their libraries, science labs, and other resources, and the attitudes and behavior of their students. In none of these important respects do they necessarily outrank institutions with lower S.A.T. averages listed in the table below, or universities and colleges not listed at all. Many institutions are, after all, left off these particular lists simply because they have more than 3,000 undergraduates. More than half the Ivy League, together with Stanford, Duke, Northwestern, and many others, are missing from these lists of small colleges for that reason.

In short, these groupings by S.A.T. score are an important clue to the level of work to expect from fellow students and therefore the kinds of standards by which one's own work will be judged. They do not represent a ranking of institutions in any other sense, but are simply one way to begin narrowing choices among small colleges so as to look closely at a few schools to see which would be a good match for the particular student. Small colleges with test scores in the 1100–1199 range are shown below—again, listed alphabetically within each region:

Combined S.A.T. 1100–1199

Northeast: Albright, Allegheny, Bates*, Colby, Connecticut, Dickinson, Drew*, Fairfield, Franklin & Marshall*, Hamilton*, Hampshire, Hobart & William Smith, Holy Cross, Mount Holyoke, St. Lawrence, Sarah Lawrence, Siena, Simon's Rock, Skidmore, Trinity (Connecticut), Yeshiva*.

South:	Furman, Millsaps, Oglethorpe, Rhodes*, Southwestern (Tennessee), University of Richmond, University of the South (Sewanee).
West:	Colorado College, Occidental*, St. John's (New Mexico), Whitman*, Willamette.
Midwest:	Albion, Case Western Reserve*, Denison, Earlham*, Grinnell*, Kalamazoo*, Kenyon*, Lawrence University, Macalester, St. Olaf, Wheaton* (Illinois).

At colleges whose average composite S.A.T.'s are in the 1100s, there is a somewhat lower proportion of institutions with 7 percent or more of their graduates continuing on to the doctorate, compared to colleges and universities with composite S.A.T.'s of 1200 and above. A sharper drop-off occurs as we move to colleges whose average S.A.T.'s are in the range from 1000 to 1099. Nevertheless, it is remarkable that a significant minority of these institutions still send this many on to receive doctorates—which puts them ahead of Berkeley, Penn, U.C.L.A., Michigan, Wisconsin, Minnesota, Texas, Northwestern, and many other large and highly rated universities.

Combined S.A.T. 1000–1099

Northeast:	Bard, Bennington, Canisius, Catholic University*, Clark, Gettysburg, Gordon, Goucher, Grove City, Hood, Houghton, Juniata, Le Moyne, Messiah, Muhlenberg, St. Joseph's (Pennsylvania), St. Mary's (Maryland), State University of New York (Purchase), Stonehill, Ursinus, Washington College (Maryland), Washington and Jefferson, Wells, Wheaton (Massachusetts).

South: Agnes Scott, Austin, Birmingham-Southern*, Centre, Eckerd*, Hampden-Sydney, Hendrix, Hollins, Mary Washington, Randolph-Macon, Randolph-Macon Woman's College, Rollins, Southwestern University (Texas), Spring Hill, Stetson, Transylvania.

West: Evergreen, Lewis & Clark, Mills, Pacific Lutheran, Pepperdine, Pitzer, Scripps, University of Denver, University of Puget Sound, University of Tulsa, Whittier.

Midwest: Alma, Antioch*, Beloit, Butler, Calvin, Coe, Concordia (Minnesota), Cornell College, DePauw, Gustavus Adolphus, Hamline, Hope*, Illinois College, John Carroll, Knox*, Lake Forest, Luther, Ohio Wesleyan, Ripon, St. Benedict, St. John's University (Minnesota), St. Mary's (Indiana), Wabash*, Westminster (Missouri), Wittenberg, Wooster*.

Liberal arts colleges with S.A.T. scores below this level are not to be written off. Some that may be well worth checking into include Hillsdale, Rockford, and Berea colleges. They would be of special interest for those seeking a more traditional education in a more conservative social environment. Nevertheless, a line had to be drawn somewhere, and it was drawn just above their current S.A.T. levels.

✔ WEEDING OUT

While each of the above listings might suggest that there are large numbers of suitable colleges available, covering a wide range of student capabilities, each list represents only a "first cut" in the process of weeding out possibilities to get to promising matches between individual and institutions. Merely looking for a school in your own geographic region shrinks each list substantially. Whether you are looking for a college with educational and social structure or one with a do-your-own-thing philosophy, either characteristic will eliminate still more of the possibilities. Depending on how many requirements you have, even the national list may shrink very quickly. This is no reason to panic. After all, you need only one college. But it is important to understand at the outset that it may take considerable time and thought to find even a few good possibilities by the time for application.

The task is by no means overwhelming, however. The longest list of small liberal arts colleges for any region and S.A.T. level is that of 25 northeastern institutions in the 1000–1099 range. If you pick up a general descriptive guide like Fiske's *Selective Guide to the Colleges* and begin reading his descriptions of their academic and social environments, you will undoubtedly begin to cross some of these 25 colleges off your list for various reasons, and perhaps take a special interest in some of those remaining. You may have only a dozen or so on the list when you turn to another guide for second opinions, or to look up colleges not covered in Fiske's guide. This process will probably further shrink the number of institutions remaining, while perhaps adding new interest or curiosity about some of the others. Whether you are looking for an experimental academic and social environment or a conservative one, an emphasis or a de-emphasis on varsity athletics, a place where fraternities and sororities abound or don't exist at all, many colleges will fall by the wayside as you go down your list.

This may sound like a lot of reading but it isn't, and of course it need not all be done at one sitting. Even if you go through three or four guides, reading only about the colleges on your list, the reading will probably amount to fewer total pages than you usually find in a single book. Knowing what you are looking for makes the task much easier.

Even those who begin with a long list of colleges extending beyond their region will probably end up with a very manageable list of a dozen or so. Those who begin with a more modest-sized list may well find themselves with too few colleges of the sort they want in their region and have to look at some more from other regions. The goal at this first stage is to end up with a list of a dozen or so institutions from which you can request brochures and catalogues for a closer look, with perhaps a few campus visits later on for those that seem especially promising after going through their literature.

✔ STRENGTHS AND WEAKNESSES

One of the problems common to small liberal arts colleges in general, their limited number of courses, is dealt with differently in different institutions. A college with many pre-med students may have a sizeable and strong chemistry department and biology department, skimping on drama, music, or art, or perhaps eliminating them entirely. Another small college, with a different kind of student body, may be heavy in drama, music, and art, and light in scientific and pre-professional fields. Such differing emphases will often be apparent in descriptions in the college guides or can be discovered in their catalogues and brochures, or by talking to people in their admissions offices. Franklin & Marshall College is not Bennington, as both will undoubtedly be anxious to make clear. Their strengths are in different areas and their goals lie in radically different directions, though both are called liberal arts colleges. The future physician or chemist at Franklin & Marshall is not looking for what the future artist or writer is seeking at Bennington.

The proportion of undergraduate degrees received in different fields is one rough indicator of where a college's strengths and weaknesses lie, but the mere granting of numerous degrees in a particular subject says little about how solidly prepared the students are in that subject. A better indicator of how well prepared the students are in different academic areas is how many are able to continue on to the doctorate in those areas. It is not just a question of the number or proportions of Ph.D.'s received by a college's graduates, but also a question of the kind of fields in which these doctorates are concentrated.

Bennington and other colleges with a reputation for a "free floating" philosophy tend generally to have small proportions of their alumni doctorates in fields like mathematics, the physical sciences, or engineering. Only 7 percent of Bennington's alumni doctorates were in any of these three fields in 1977–1986 and the proportions were similarly modest at Bard College (10%), Sarah Lawrence (1%), and Evergreen State (11%). This contrasts with proportions two or three times as high at more traditional colleges such as Amherst (23%) or the University of Chicago (23%). Proportions are even higher at some colleges with a scientific or technological orientation, such as Franklin & Marshall (30%), Union College (34%), or Lafayette College (40%).

Again, specific numbers are not crucial. What is important is to recognize that colleges differ radically in where their strengths lie. Because some of the smaller liberal arts colleges may not be able to cover all the fields equally well, it is important to be sure that their strengths match your interests. Bryn Mawr College, for example, is number one in the nation in the percentage of its students who continue on to Ph.D.'s in the humanities, but it is not even among the top 50 in the percentage receiving Ph.D.'s in mathematics, the physical sciences, and engineering. By the same token, none of the technical institutes like Harvey Mudd, Cal Tech, or M.I.T. is among the top 50 in percentage of students going on to receive humanities doctorates—nor, for that matter, are such strong scientific liberal arts colleges as Lafayette, Union, and Franklin & Marshall.

The fact that some liberal arts colleges are far stronger in some areas than in others—as some universities are as well—does not imply that liberal arts colleges in general are lopsided. Many small liberal arts colleges are strong simultaneously in the humanities, the social sciences, mathematics, and the physical and biological sciences. Indeed, among 17 institutions with the highest proportions of their graduates receiving doctorates in all these fields *simultaneously*, 14 are small liberal arts colleges. In alphabetical order, these 17 institutions are: Amherst, Antioch, Carleton, Chicago, Grinnell, Harvard, Haverford, Kalamazoo, New College, Oberlin, Pomona, Reed, U.C. Riverside, Swarthmore, Wesleyan (Connecticut), and Wooster.

Like all the other lists, this is not intended to be a ranking of the "best." It is intended to convey some important information that may be useful to you in trying to match your interests and talents with the right college for you. If you are not sure whether your main interests will be in the humanities, the sciences, or elsewhere, then colleges with top-quality programs across the board may be of special interest to you. Even if you do have some idea where your general interests are concentrated, you may still want a college that is very strong in the other fields as well. On the other hand, if your interests are wholly in the humanities, Bryn Mawr may be perfect for you (assuming many other things match), just as Union or Lafayette may be tailor-made for someone whose interests are strongly focussed on science and technology.

Some liberal arts colleges located in the vicinity of other colleges and universities make up for the limited range of courses at one institution by allowing students from one college to take some courses at neighboring institutions. In Massachusetts, for example, Amherst, Smith, Mount Holyoke, Hampshire, and the University of Massachusetts have such a cooperative arrangement with one another. In California, Pomona, Claremont McKenna, Pitzer, Scripps, and Harvey Mudd colleges not only have a similar arrangement but are also located within walking distance of each other. Smaller groups of colleges elsewhere have such reciprocal arrangements, including pairs of colleges like St. Olaf and Carleton, both located in Northfield, Minnesota. Some of the institutions that do this are strong across the board, and cooperate simply to make more options available to their own students and those of neighboring institutions. In other cases, however, a cooperative arrangement enables a college (or university or engineering school) to cover an area in which it might otherwise be weak.

Where a college is located far from any comparable institution, like Whitman College in southeastern Washington state or Wabash College in rural Indiana, it must be judged by its own resources alone. Seldom will these resources match those of a large university in absolute terms. However, what matters is whether these resources are adequate—or ample—for the number of students they serve. In terms of endowment per student, for example, both Whitman and Wabash have more than Columbia University, and so have the money to offer strong programs on their own. Obviously, endowment is not the only consideration, even financially. But the point is that the basis of whatever comparison is made must be *per student*. More important, the things that you are interested in need to be checked out specifically for each institution, whether it is computers, biology labs, or anything else.

Some liberal arts colleges are in financial straits and it shows in their equipment, libraries, and faculty. Others are in robust financial health. The same wide variations occur among universities. The big universities, of course, have the largest endowments in absolute amounts. However, in terms of college endowment *per student*, only 4 of the top 10 belong to colleges at universities (Princeton, Harvard, Yale, Stanford) and 6 belong to independent liberal arts colleges (Swarthmore, Wabash, Williams, Dartmouth, Carleton, and Oberlin).

Whether measured by resources or results, liberal arts colleges more than hold their own with universities at all academic levels when it comes to educating undergraduates. Universities, of course, often have larger goals, including major research and the training of graduate students, physicians, and lawyers. However, undergraduate education is what matters when you are choosing a college.

CHAPTER 4

SPECIALIZED INSTITUTIONS

Many institutions of higher education do not fall neatly into the two categories of universities and liberal arts colleges. Engineering schools like M.I.T. and Cal Tech are the most obvious and most numerous examples. The military service academies at West Point, Annapolis, and Colorado Springs (Air Force) are other clear exceptions. There are also highly specialized institutions like the Colorado School of Mines and the G.M.I. Engineering and Management Institute (formerly known as the General Motors Institute and still sponsored by that corporation). For music, there is the Juilliard School, the Eastman School of Music at the University of Rochester, and the Conservatory of Music at Oberlin. Although all these institutions are top flight in their own respective ways, they will be of interest only to those already committed—or prepared to become committed—to the specialized careers to which they lead. For some people, these careers can be very rewarding, personally and otherwise.

The demands are also very high and the competition

tough at these places, though in different ways. At M.I.T., Cal Tech, and the three military service academies, the combined S.A.T. scores of the students average 1200 or better, and at G.M.I. and the Colorado School of Mines the average is just barely below that level. None of these five institutions averages below 650 on the math S.A.T.

✔ ENGINEERING

General Education

Many engineering schools, whether separate or belonging to universities, put such emphasis on math, science, and technology that their students have little time, energy, or interest left for the other subjects that go to make up a well-rounded education. This can be a permanent loss. On the other hand, some students have no real intellectual interests outside the math and science areas, and forcing them to take many liberal arts courses may accomplish nothing besides generating frustration. For such individuals the institute of technology may be perfect. It is, however, possible to become both an engineer and an educated human being.

M.I.T. has made a real effort to ensure that its students acquire an education outside their traditional math, science, and technology areas. M.I.T.'s economics department, for example, has long been among the top handful in the nation, led by the winner of the first Nobel Prize in economics, Paul Samuelson. Some other engineering schools are trying to follow suit, with varying degrees of success. Others, like the Florida Institute of Technology, are unabashedly in business to train people for careers in some narrowly specialized areas such as photographic technology or oceanic engineering.

A compromise which some may find attractive is to take three years at a liberal arts college that has a special arrangement with some engineering school to which the student then transfers for two years of pure engineering before receiving a degree. These "3–2" programs are very widespread. About 500 institutions are involved, including many outstanding liberal arts colleges and top engineering schools. You cannot, however, simply go to your favorite liberal arts college for three years and then automatically transfer to your favorite engineering school.

The 3–2 programs involve highly specific links between particular colleges and particular tech schools. Oberlin, for example, has 3–2 programs with the engineering schools at Case Western Reserve and at Washington University in St. Louis. Whitman College has 3–2 programs with Cal Tech and with engineering schools at Duke and Columbia. Franklin & Marshall is 3–2 with Columbia, Georgia Tech, Rensselaer, and Washington University in St. Louis. Anyone planning a 3–2 program must not only make the usual match between student and institution but with two institutions—and then make sure that those two institutions are linked to each other. There are also some liberal arts colleges, such as Swarthmore and Lafayette, which have their own engineering programs and award their own engineering degrees.

Lists and Rankings

Because there are so many ways of acquiring an engineering degree—from colleges, universities, technical institutes, and military academies—the problems of comparing and choosing are complicated, and the problems of

making objective rankings are practically impossible. Moreover, engineering schools give degrees in subjects other
than engineering—not only in mathematics and the physical
sciences but also in some cases business management, economics, or even in the humanities.

With engineering schools, as with liberal arts colleges,
some outstanding institutions may be little known to the
general public beyond their region, or even within their
region. However, they are likely to be known to those who
matter to your career as an engineer, whether these are
employers of engineers or officials of graduate schools of
engineering. Everyone has heard of M.I.T. and Cal Tech,
but most laymen would be surprised to learn that Harvey
Mudd College has a higher percentage of its graduates go
on to receive doctorates than either of these renowned institutions. Many would be surprised that Cooper Union
comes next among engineering schools in this respect.

Engineering schools that belong to universities may
take on the prestige (or lack of prestige) of these universities in the eyes of the general public. However, that can
be very misleading as a basis for making your own choices.
For example, in chemical engineering the University of
Delaware has been ranked by the profession among the top
10 institutions in the nation, ahead of M.I.T. and Princeton,
though it is not as highly rated in civil engineering, electrical engineering, or mechanical engineering, and of course
is not nearly as well known in general. These rankings, like
most rankings of universities, reflect the research of the
graduate faculty.

The point here is that it makes no more sense to look
simply for the "top 10" in engineering than in any other
field when choosing what school to apply to. It is instead a
question of matching your own interests and qualifications.

If your overriding interest is in chemical engineering, the University of Delaware may be for you. At the very least, it should not be dismissed simply because you were accepted somewhere else with a more widely known name. People who know the field of chemical engineering will know about the University of Delaware.

While rankings of institutions do not tell you what is crucial—how well a given place suits your own interests and qualifications—some rankings can be useful simply as a source of information about colleges, universities, or technical institutes you may never have thought of otherwise. As long as these rankings are not taken as the last word, but only as a first step toward looking into various possibilities, they can be useful.

Many students who are considering engineering as a career have not absolutely fixed on engineering but are interested in the general area of mathematics, the physical sciences, and technology. For such students, a ranking of those colleges, universities, and technical institutes with the highest percentage of their graduates going on to receive doctorates in math, the physical sciences, and engineering can be one of these useful lists:

Institution	%
1. Harvey Mudd College	34.4
2. California Institute of Technology	33.7
3. Massachusetts Institute of Technology	17.3
4. Cooper Union for the Advancement of Science and Art	12.5
5. Webb Institute of Naval Architecture	11.0
6. Reed College	8.7
7. Rice University	8.0
8. Rensselaer Polytechnic Institute	7.3
9. Polytechnic Institute of New York	7.2

10. Carnegie-Mellon University   6.8
11. University of Chicago   6.5
12. University of California at San Diego   5.5
13. New Mexico Institute of Mining   5.5
14. Swarthmore College   5.2
15. Worcester Polytechnic Institute   5.2
16. Stevens Institute of Technology   5.0
17. Colorado School of Mines   4.9
18. Haverford College   4.9
19. Harvard College   4.6
20. Illinois Institute of Technology   4.5
21. Princeton University   4.5
22. South Dakota School of Mines   4.4
23. Johns Hopkins University   4.2
24. Case Western Reserve University   4.1
25. Carleton College   4.0
26. Rose-Hulman Institute of Technology   4.0
27. Lehigh University   3.9
28. New College of the University of South Florida   3.9
29. Pomona College   3.7
30. Illinois Benedictine   3.6

Source: Change, Nov./Dec. 1986

Obviously, these numbers and percentages do *not* represent quality rankings. The University of Chicago teaches many things besides math and science, while the Webb Institute of Naval Architecture is even more narrowly focussed than most engineering schools. The fact that a higher percentage of the Webb Institute's students go on for doctorates in math, science, or engineering does not make it superior to the University of Chicago, even within these areas. Given the heterogeneous make-up of these institutions, what is important—and in some cases, surprising—is who is on the list, not their exact ranking. If you would not have thought of Rensselaer or the Rose-Hulman Institute without this list, nor thought of Harvey Mudd as in any way comparable to M.I.T. or Cal Tech, then the list has been useful to that extent.

Universities with strong math, science, and engineering programs may fail to make a list like this simply because they have students in so many other fields. Ideally, we would like quality rankings of math, science, and engineering departments at undergraduate institutions. Nothing like that exists and it is doubtful if anyone has the knowledge to create such rankings. The closest we can come are quality rankings of graduate departments. This is easier to do, because the professors in the leading graduate departments are known to colleagues around the country through their publications. The profession knows where the top scholars in the field are, even if they don't know how well they teach undergraduates. Once you understand this limitation, you may be able to make use of the following lists of leading departments in various fields of science and technology:

Computer Science
1. Stanford
2. M.I.T.
3. Carnegie-Mellon
4. Berkeley
5.* U.C.L.A.
5.* University of Illinois
7. University of Washington
8.* Univ. of Southern California
8.* University of Texas
10. University of Wisconsin

Chemical Engineering
1. University of Minnesota
2. University of Wisconsin
3. Cal Tech
4. Berkeley
5. Stanford
6. University of Delaware
7. M.I.T.
8. University of Houston
9.* University of Illinois
9.* Princeton

Electrical Engineering	*Civil Engineering*
1. M.I.T.	1. Berkeley
2.* Berkeley	2. M.I.T.
2.* Stanford	3. University of Illinois
4. University of Illinois	4. Cal Tech
5.* U.C.L.A.	5. University of Texas
5.* Univ. of Southern California	6. Stanford
7. Cornell	7. Cornell
8. Purdue	8.* Northwestern
9. Cal Tech	8.* Purdue
10. Princeton	10. University of Michigan

*Tied in ranking.

Source: Conference Board of Associated Research Councils

If these lists of the top graduate departments seem to have relatively little overlap with the undergraduate institutions listed before, that is very similar to what happens in other areas of education. The big universities dominate at the graduate level, in many fields, while their own undergraduates are often not as likely to complete graduate training for the Ph.D. as the undergraduates from smaller institutions. Harvey Mudd, Cooper Union, and Rose-Hulman are all missing from these four lists of leading graduate engineering departments simply because these three are all undergraduate institutions.

All these lists have blind spots. Lists may be able to help you in your thinking but they can never be a substitute for that thinking.

In engineering, as in other fields, ranking institutions is far less important than matching individuals with institutions. Here again, your test scores provide one rough way to begin the sorting process. Because mathematics is so central to engineering, it makes sense to group institutes of technology by quantitative S.A.T. scores rather than by composite S.A.T.'s.

Within each grouping below, the schools are in alphabetical order, as before. Universities are listed only where they have separate undergraduate engineering schools, and the quantitative S.A.T. scores used for grouping them are the scores solely for these engineering schools, regardless of what S.A.T. scores may be elsewhere in the university. This list therefore omits some highly regarded engineering programs, such as those at Rice, Bucknell, Stanford, and Swarthmore, which are not separate from the regular undergraduate programs at these institutions, and so could not be grouped separately as the others are.

Quantitative S.A.T.'s in the 700s

Northeast: Carnegie-Mellon, Columbia, Cooper Union, Cornell, M.I.T., Princeton, University of Pennsylvania

South: Duke University

West: Cal Tech, Harvey Mudd, University of California (Berkeley)

Midwest: ———

It is hardly surprising that there are so few institutions with average math S.A.T.'s in the 700s. It is remarkable that there are as many as there are, and anyone considering applying to any of these places should be certain that he or she is prepared for a school whose other students have such extraordinary mathematical ability. There needs to be a similar caution concerning some of the institutions listed below, specifically those whose average S.A.T.'s are in the upper 600s, only marginally less than those shown above.

Quantitative S.A.T.'s in the 600s

Northeast: Alfred University, Boston University, Clarkson, Drexel, George Washington University (D.C.), Lehigh, Penn State, Polytechnic Institute of N.Y., Rensselaer Polytechnic, Rutgers (New Brunswick), Stevens Institute, Syracuse, Tufts, University of Connecticut, University of Delaware, University of Maryland (College Park), University of Massachusetts (Amherst), University of Pittsburgh, Valparaiso, Villanova, Webb Institute, Worcester Polytechnic.

South: Georgia Tech, North Carolina State University (Raleigh), Tulane, University of Florida, University of Houston, University of Miami, University of Texas (Austin), University of Virginia, Vanderbilt, Virginia Polytechnic, West Virginia University.

West: Colorado School of Mines, Colorado State University, Oregon State University, Santa Clara University, South Dakota School of Mines and Technology, University of California (Santa Barbara), University of Washington (Seattle).

Midwest: Case Western Reserve, G.M.I. Institute, Michigan Technological University, Northwestern, Notre Dame, Purdue, Rose-Hulman Institute, University of Cincinnati, University of Illinois (Urbana), University of Minnesota (Minneapolis), University of Michigan (Ann Arbor), University of Missouri (Rolla), University of Wisconsin (Madison), Washington University (St. Louis).

Although colleges and universities tend to become more numerous as you go down the test score range, engineering schools seem to become more scarce at quantitative S.A.T. levels below 600. There are some engineering schools with math S.A.T.'s in the 500s, however, and some of these are well-thought-of. As with institutions from any list, they need to be investigated individually.

Quantitative S.A.T.'s in the 500s

Northeast: New Jersey Institute of Technology, Pratt Institute, Rochester Institute of Technology.

South: Clemson, Florida Institute of Technology, Texas A&M, University of Central Florida, University of Kentucky, University of Mississippi, University of South Carolina, University of Texas (Arlington).

West: California Polytechnic State University (San Luis Obispo), Montana College of Mineral Science and Technology, New Mexico Institute of Mining and Technology, Northrup University, University of Arizona, University of Idaho.

Midwest: Illinois Institute of Technology, Indiana Institute of Technology, Marquette, Milwaukee School of Engineering, Ohio State, University of Evansville, University of Missouri (Columbia), University of Wisconsin (Milwaukee).

Specialization

In addition to the same problem of trying to match the individual with the institution, which applies when choosing a liberal arts college or a university, engineering students face additional decisions. Because engineering is so specialized, often a choice must be made fairly early in your college career as to whether to take the sequence of courses required for chemical engineering rather than mechanical engineering, electrical engineering, or other specialties. Early and perhaps premature commitments are among the dangers facing those who go into engineering. That means that it is worth considering while still in high school that a decision to go to an engineering school narrows your future choices in a way that those choices are not narrowed by going to a college or university where you can leave your options open to major in math or physics, for example, if you should discover that your real interest is there rather than in applied fields of engineering.

The value of being able to leave your options open varies with how decided or undecided you are right now. But even if you feel pretty sure that you want to become an engineer, and perhaps what kind of engineer, it is still advisable to find out beforehand how easy or how difficult it would be to change after a year in one program. If the college catalogue does not make that clear, a letter or telephone call to the admissions office should clear it up—and is well worth the trouble.

✔ MILITARY ACADEMIES

Even more than engineering schools, military academies require a heavy commitment of time, emotion, and energy focussed on a narrow area while in school, and a commitment to a specific career afterwards. West Point is more than a place to go to school. It is a way of life, intended to leave its mark indelibly, even under the later stress of life-and-death situations. The same is true of the U.S. Naval Academy at Annapolis, the U.S. Air Force Academy in Colorado, and the Coast Guard Academy in Connecticut. Nowhere is it more important to be sure that you match the institution when choosing a college.

The military service academies are, of course, meant to be more than academic institutions. However, the quality of their academic foundation may be indicated by the fact that West Point alumni received 79 doctorates in engineering alone during the decade from 1977 to 1986. This was more than the number of engineering doctorates received during the same period by the alumni of Johns Hopkins, Duke, Harvard, or Yale. Altogether, West Pointers received more than 300 doctorates in all fields during this decade—a remarkable achievement for an institution designed primarily to produce military officers capable of leading troops in combat. It is also remarkable for an institution whose faculty are mostly military officers without Ph.D.'s themselves.

Like most institutions that turn out outstanding people, West Point takes in outstanding people. Only about 10 percent of those who apply are accepted, and 10 percent of these are high school valedictorians. Three-quarters scored above 600 on the mathematics S.A.T. Small class sizes and gruelling hours of work do the rest.

Despite a physically, emotionally, and intellectually taxing pace that the Military Academy itself characterizes as "total involvement," 70 percent of the entering cadets survive to graduate. After their required five years in the Army, about three-quarters of West Pointers volunteer to continue a military career.

Much the same story could be told of the other military service academies. More than 30 percent of the class of 1991 at Annapolis scored in the 700s on the math S.A.T. Four-fifths ranked in the top 20 percent of their high school classes. The Naval Academy boasts among its alumni more than two dozen Rhodes Scholars, a Nobel Prize winner, astronauts, and a President of the United States. (West Point alumni include presidents Grant and Eisenhower.) Graduates of the Naval Academy may become officers either in the Navy or the Marine Corps.

The Air Force Academy in Colorado Springs has aca-

demic and other standards very similar to those of West
Point and Annapolis. About three-quarters of its graduates
become either pilots or navigators. The Coast Guard,
though a part of the Navy during wartime, has its own
separate service academy in New London, Connecticut.
Less than 10 percent of its applicants are admitted.

The attractions of the military service academies—a
high-quality education free, with living expenses paid by
the government, and a career waiting at graduation—bring
vast numbers of applications. This enables the academies
to screen not only for academic qualifications but also for
stringent physical requirements. As the application process
requires nomination by a member of Congress, more time
is required than for applying to most colleges.

In addition to the academies run by the military services
themselves, there are also unaffiliated military academies
such as the Virginia Military Institute and the Citadel, both
state-supported. The federal government's Merchant Marine Academy on Long Island, New York, is quasi-military
and its graduates may become naval officers as well as officers in the civilian merchant marine. The Maine Maritime
Academy is a state-supported institution which also trains
students to become officers in the merchant marine. The
academic standards of the non-affiliated academies in general do not match those of the four major service academies,
though they may offer a good education. But it is not clear
whether they offer any advantages over entering a military
career from a Reserve Officers Training Corps (ROTC) at
a conventional college.

CHAPTER 5

KINDS OF EDUCATION

Education varies in many ways—in the way it is organized (the curriculum), in the effectiveness with which the material is taught, and in the quality of the instructor's own understanding of the material. All of these vary enormously, from professor to professor and from college to college. What also varies enormously is the seriousness with which teaching is done—and the honesty. All these things require careful attention when choosing a college, and most are not immediately obvious to the naked eye, but require thoughtful consideration beforehand to know what to look for.

✔ THE CURRICULUM

Course Requirements
Contrasting approaches to the curriculum can be found at all academic levels and in all parts of the country. Two Florida institutions illustrate these differences. At the

Florida Institute of Technology, most baccalaureate programs "are completely outlined for each discipline," according to the school itself. When you decide to become a chemical engineer, the institution prescribes exactly what courses you need to achieve that goal, and these courses leave little room for any electives chosen by the student. At New College, however, your program of courses "is something you fashion in response to your experiences, the counsel you receive from faculty and other students." Whether you take all your courses in one narrow area or wander at random among the whole range of courses offered is your decision. As the school itself says:

> To be candid, you run the risk at New College that you will over-specialize or that you will omit from your program some curriculum component that you will later wish you had obtained. But as a New College student you have the advantage of knowing that your education is truly *your* education, with all the challenge and excitement implied.

How much of an "advantage" that is is open to question. While many would agree that experience is indeed the crucial factor needed to plan an educational program, probably fewer would agree with the assumption that an 18-year-old has enough of this experience to determine what he or she will or will not need for the next half century or so of a life and a career. Nor is consultation with other inexperienced classmates much of a solution. It is like trying to draw a map of a road you have never travelled. According to the philosophy of New College, those who have travelled the road are only to offer advice—and this only from faculty, with parents totally ignored. However, New College is by no means alone in this approach.

For opposite reasons, neither New College nor the Florida Institute of Technology has "distribution requirements" prescribing a diversity of general areas (science, humanities, etc.) that a student must study. Most colleges have distribution requirements but they vary in how these requirements are administered. If a science requirement can be met by taking psychology rather than physics, then the curriculum means much less in practice than in theory. If "exceptions" are granted freely, then the rule means nothing. Whether you prefer a curriculum that is strict or loose, it needs to be checked out by a careful reading of the college catalogue and by asking questions about it in person if you make a campus visit. "How hard is it to get exceptions?" is a good question to put to college officials—and to students. Their answers may differ.

My own view is that those who have travelled the road need to guide those who have not. Only in a few fields like engineering does this need to mean specification of each course. But a liberal arts education means equipping a person for life—which is to say, for many unknown contingencies, like a soldier preparing to go into battle. No one knows exactly how the battle will go, but those who have been through many battles should know some of the basic requirements. You can't go in unarmed, or with no means of caring for wounds, or with nothing to eat or drink—or with no discipline.

As an undergraduate, I despised French and crammed to pass a comprehensive examination which exempted me from having to take any more courses in the subject. It was a great relief to be rid of it. But, a decade later, my research required me to read five volumes in French because the material I needed was simply not available in English. Nearly 20 years after that, while studying an entirely different field, I once again found that the key information I needed was available only in a study published in French and never translated. As an undergraduate deciding whether or not to study French, I had no inkling of the topics I would be working on in future decades, much less whether or not they would require reading French. A student is usually in no position to judge "relevance" until years later, when it is far too late.

The abandonment of distribution requirements—and many other academic rules—that has occurred in many places since the 1960s may reflect changing opinions on the curriculum. It may also in some cases reflect simply an abdication of responsibility by colleges and universities. Students may be allowed to "do their own thing" simply because that is the path of least resistance for academic administrators and faculty members.

Not all colleges without formal distribution requirements have abandoned students to their fate, nor are all students going to take an unrelated scattering of courses if permitted to. The later academic success of New College students—a higher percentage go on to Ph.D.'s than do students at Yale or Stanford—suggests that some very serious and responsible thought goes into their individual programs. But this cannot be assumed everywhere.

Just as distribution requirements mean less when exceptions are permitted, so an absence of distribution requirements may mean less when faculty advice is both given and taken responsibly. In both cases, it is necessary to look beyond the immediate formalities.

"Interdisciplinary" Fields

Another important trend in recent years has been the growth and proliferation of so-called "interdisciplinary" courses and majors. There are very few truly interdisciplinary courses such as physical chemistry (which requires mastery of the principles of physics and the principles of chemistry) or econometrics (which requires mastery of the principles of economics and the principles of statistical analysis). Most of what are called "interdisciplinary" courses and majors are in fact *non*-disciplinary. In some places, you can major in Southeast Asian Studies but Southeast Asia is a geographic region, not a set of intellectual principles like mathematics or logic. If you studied the Balkans instead, you would be using the same intellectual processes.

To confuse a subject matter (however fascinating) with an intellectual discipline is to undermine the whole point of an education. Mere information can be gotten from any almanac or encyclopedia. An education includes a discipline, a structured way of thinking. Mathematics is not just a subject matter; it is a particular way of organizing your thinking. A mathematician and an interior decorator can both talk about space, but they talk about it in different ways.

Classes in some of the newer "interdisciplinary" fields like ethnic studies or women's studies have become notorious for degenerating into "rap sessions." That seldom happens in physics or chemistry because these are disciplines with an inherent structure of their own.

This is not an argument against studying certain subjects. There has been outstanding scholarship and teaching on the subject of black Americans, for example, for decades before the first Black Studies department was created. More than half a century ago, such distinguished scholars as Carter G. Woodson did studies on the subject as an historian, E. Franklin Frazier as a sociologist, and Abram L. Harris as an economist. Each had his own discipline and taught in a corresponding department to students learning the respective discipline. None of them taught courses that could be described as an Afro-American Studies seminar at Princeton was described in the *Student Course Guide* there as "simply a 3-hour 'rap session' "—one where there were "few students who did the assigned readings" and where the grading was "arbitrary" and "random." Other courses in the same department received similar comments.

Such comments apply to many such courses in other places besides Princeton, and in other "interdisciplinary" fields besides Afro-American Studies. "Women's Studies," "Environmental Studies," or "Peace Studies," can likewise all be taught either as rap sessions or as serious exercises in some particular discipline—which is to say that none of them is itself a discipline, much less a combination of disciplines.

It is not the subject matter of a course but its intellectual structure that determines whether or not it is part of some discipline. At Stanford, for example, a course called "Race and Ethnic Relations" is listed as part of its program in African and Afro-American Studies, but it is still Sociology 145—in concept as well as in name. The heavyweight readings make it clear that this is no rap session. But, in case anyone misses the message, the syllabus states on the first page that this course is about "explaining phenomena in a rigorous, scientific sense," that mere "empathy" for this or that group is not the point. Anyone familiar with the professor who teaches the course is unlikely to think that this is mere talk. He is teaching a course in his discipline.

The point of all this is that the label "interdisciplinary" covers such a wide range of possibilities as to be almost meaningless. Where it is literally true—where the intellectual principles of two or more fields are used in combination—there are likely to be very difficult and demanding courses, like physical chemistry or econometrics. But the term is seldom used in this sense by those advocating "interdisciplinary" studies. All too often, so-called "interdisciplinary" courses and programs represent an abandonment of any discipline, substituting enthusiasm for some subject or for some ideologically preconceived conclusions about that subject. It is these kinds of "interdisciplinary" courses which lend themselves to becoming rap sessions among the true believers. A third possibility—a program which simply includes courses drawn from a variety of specific disciplines—can more readily escape this fate, but that program does not itself constitute a discipline, and a degree in such a program would indicate little or nothing about the student's mastery of some intellectual process.

From a practical point of view, what matters about a college with many "interdisciplinary" programs and majors is just what kind of courses these are in reality. It matters not only to those who intend to take these courses but also to those who don't. A college which abdicates its responsibility to students by setting up phoney "rap session" courses is a college whose commitment to education in general may be questionable.

The best way to find out whether these courses are for real is to ask students and faculty members *from other fields* during a campus visit. You can expect more candid answers, the more you are able to question each individual privately and "off the record." Students and faculty from more traditional fields, especially fields with a demanding intellectual structure of their own (chemistry, math, economics), are in an especially good position to tell you whether the "interdisciplinary" courses have real structure and substance. Even when you have to ask your questions in a group, if the answer is hesitant, tense, and phrased in weasel words, that sometimes tells you all you need to know—especially if the same person has been very glib in giving you answers to other questions.

✔ TEACHING

Like brain surgery, teaching is one of those things that can go on right before your eyes without your really understanding what is happening. Everyone who is ready for college has already seen so many teachers that familiarity may create a false sense of understanding.

Some aspects of teaching can be readily understood, and these are sometimes important aspects. A teacher who is chronically late for class, unprepared, impatient with questions, and disorganized in presentation is clearly bad news. There are too many professors like that, at all academic levels, including some of the most prestigious universities. You can spot these kinds of professors with the naked eye, and you should make a note of how many of them you encounter when you sit in on various college classes during a campus visit.

Most students try to avoid such professors like the plague, so there is only a limited amount of damage they can do. A much more serious threat to education is the fluent, interesting, perhaps even charismatic, professor who fundamentally misconceives his own subject. He can attract students in droves—and pass on his confusions to class after class, year after year. Such professors may get rave reviews from students because anyone who already understood the subject well enough to judge would have no reason to take the course. Only those few students who continue on to more advanced levels in the same field are likely to have any way to reassess what they were taught—and this reassessment may occur years after they have graduated. By then, of course, it will do them no good, nor will it help students still being fed the great performer's misconceptions.

One of the most important tasks of a teacher takes place long before the first class meeting. This is canvassing the vast material that might possibly be presented to determine what small fraction of it is crucial, and structuring its presentation to maximize the student's understanding of the subject. Students are not present while this is going on and would not know how to judge how well the professor did this job if they were. When I taught labor economics at Douglass College a quarter of a century ago, one of my students was a young lady whose boy friend was also taking labor economics at Princeton. They discovered that there was absolutely no overlap between the two courses. She seemed astonished that courses with the same name did not have a single topic in common.

Knowing who taught labor economics at Princeton at that time, I was not the least bit surprised. But the students were not only puzzled but disturbed. More important, they had no way of knowing which of us had completely misconceived what labor economics was all about. The kind of labor economics taught at Princeton at that time has long since disappeared, not only at Princeton but elsewhere as well. But unless these students went on to postgraduate work in economics, or otherwise kept in touch with the field for some special reason, they probably do not understand, to this moment, why the two courses were so different.

This is not an unusual situation. For example, one of the leading lights in the economics of industrial organization teaches at Swarthmore College. But his syllabus contains no assigned readings from economists who are leading lights in the opposite school of thought in industrial organization—which happens to be a school of thought that is displacing his. All that the Swarthmore students can judge is how well their professor conducts his class and how interesting the readings are that he assigns. If they had a copy of the syllabus for industrial organization as it is taught at Rice, Princeton, or the University of Washington, they might discover an entirely different perspective on the subject. But seldom, if ever, are the students at any institution able to assess a course in terms of what has been left out—and yet that may be the most important fact about the course.

Indoctrination and Irresponsibility

One-sided presentations are the rule rather than the exception in some fields or in some subjects, such as Marxism, race, feminism, or "peace studies." An all too common pattern is that found in a course called "Introduction to Marxian Economics" at the University of Texas in Austin. The syllabus is full of the writings of Marx and Engels and latter-day Marxists—but not one writing from any of the many critics of Marxism. According to the syllabus: "The course as a whole provides you with an opportunity to learn how to view the world from a new point of view and the tests are aimed at evaluating whether and to what degree you have learned to do this." In short, it is not Marxism that is to be examined critically, but the United States and the world through Marxist eyes—and the student is to be graded on how well he or she does that. Moreover, this requirement is termed an "opportunity"!

This approach is by no means peculiar to this particular

course at the University of Texas. At many institutions, courses on Marxism are taught by Marxists, some of whom openly admit that how well the student learns to criticize American society from a Marxian perspective determines the grade that will be given. They profess to see nothing wrong with this, either intellectually or ethically. According to a New York University Marxist professor, "a correct understanding of Marxism (or any body of scientific thought) leads automatically to its acceptance."

The question is not whether the professor, the student, or the parent likes Marxism. The question is whether teaching has been betrayed by being turned into indoctrination.

The same question can be asked in other areas and at all too many other institutions. The Harvard Students' *Confidential Guide* describes lectures in a course called "Women and the Law" as containing a "shallow, one-sided description of the facts of the cases, the lawyers' arguments, the feminist perspective, and little else." The course provides "little opportunity for debate or original thinking." Propaganda courses often give easy grades to attract a following, and this course seems to fit the pattern: "It's virtually impossible to do badly when exam time comes around," according to *The Confidential Guide*, and the term paper "can be about any topic you can think of that is even remotely related to the course's topic."

Similarly, at Dartmouth, a music class that features the professor's rambling political commentary, expressed in abusive obscenities, is also considered "a notable gut." At American University in Washington, D.C., a professor was let go after it became known that he allowed students to grade themselves in his ideologically oriented course.

Another dimension of teaching is responsibility—something that should be taken for granted but cannot be.

Irresponsible self-indulgence by professors takes many forms. A Harvard professor who wastes most of a geology lecture talking about the World Series and wastes other lectures on similar irrelevancies represents just one of these forms. The Harvard Students' *Confidential Guide* says of his course: "You will be going to the most expensive theater show of your life—a couple thousand bucks to watch a famous guy stroke his ego in front of 300 students."

A biology professor at the University of Texas at Austin is described in the September 1987 issue of *Texas Review*, a student publication, as "prone to spontaneous outbursts about nearly *anything* with no relation to the previous subject." He "tends to ramble" and often "degenerates into vulgarity," suggesting "a dirty old man." Another biology professor there "starts every class by playing his favorite ditties (by Gershwin and Brubeck) to the students while waddling sleepily across the stage." He suddenly "without warning" turns on "eye-popping slides of female genitalia onto the cinema-sized screen," making such accompanying remarks as "this is not my wife" and "I did not take these pictures, ha, ha."

Another University of Texas professor, in history, has a different kind of self-indulgence—using sewer language, which he then leads his class in repeating, as he vents his anger over current political issues, while supposedly teaching the pre–Civil War history of the United States. According to the *Texas Review*, a whole week was taken up showing the class slides of poverty-stricken Americans taken during the Great Depression, even though this was hardly in the pre–Civil War era. Chronology meant little in a course which "lacked continuity and consistency," where the professor went on "talking about various subjects at whim," and where a whole lecture period was spent denouncing the Reagan administration's foreign policy—again, in a course on the pre–Civil War era.

At Arizona State University, the difference between what a political science course was supposed to cover and what it actually consisted of was even greater. According to the catalogue description, the course was about political ideologies, such as conservativism, liberalism, and Marxism. But, according to students who actually took the course, it consisted primarily of the professor's own antinuclear views, together with his concerns over the environment and population. Only one of six books required for the course dealt with political ideologies at all, most of the others being anti-nuclear or environmentalist tracts. The class was also shown two movies on nuclear war. The issue is not the merits of this professor's opinions, but the bait-and-switch advertising of a course on one subject when in fact it was on an entirely different subject.

Not all irresponsible self-indulgence by professors goes to this extreme or is so obviously ideological indoctrination. But when a course on American history at Knox College assigns a futuristic novel by Edward Bellamy and parts of another novel, *The Wizard of Oz*, you know that something is wrong. Anyone familiar with Bellamy's novel knows that it does not even pretend to deal with history but is simply his vision of what a socialist Utopia would be like. This thinly disguised political tract is also required reading in American history at Franklin & Marshall College.

One of my most painful experiences during campus visits was listening to a completely one-sided presentation of the role of women in the labor force in a class on American history at Willamette University in Oregon. Not a word said, by professor or students, suggested any awareness that there were alternative views or counter-evidence on

any of the issues under discussion. One or two true believers enthusiastically supplied whatever class discussion
there was, while the other students sat in utter silence with
blank expressions. It had all the earmarks of propaganda
and passive resistance. On many campuses, those out of
step with the prevailing ideology learn early on that it is
taboo to challenge the anointed. (Not all classes at Willamette were like this. The syllabus for one economics course
featured several assignments each from John Kenneth Galbraith and Milton Friedman, which is about as diverse as
you can get.)

Many of the examples of ideological indoctrination involve professors on the political left, which leads to much
confused and misleading rhetoric about "liberal bias" on the
one hand or "McCarthyism" on the other. At this particular
juncture in history, the great majority of professors are
politically liberal or left, so that if you counted faculty members who use contact lenses or wear blue suits, most would
turn out to be liberal or left, though that has nothing to do
with contact lenses or clothing. The professor's opinions are
his own business; his behavior in class is what others have
a right to be concerned with—and, in some cases, outraged
about.

Where the teaching itself is done competently, responsibly, and honestly, the professor's opinions are irrelevant,
whether those opinions be conservative, liberal, or Marxist.
For example, liberal professors at the University of California at San Diego receive high praise from the conservative student newspaper there. Not only are individual liberal professors described by the conservative *California
Review* as "well respected," or "a great teacher"; the
faculty as a whole is complimented for its fair-mindedness:
"Papers and essays with a rightward tilt have been evalu-

ated fairly and equally to the assignments of left-leaning students," according to the *California Review*. Its "worst professor on campus award" went not to an ideological foe but to a professor of physics whose English was hard to understand and whose math was often wrong.

The conservative *Texas Review* likewise gave praise in its September 1987 issue to some liberal-left professors and criticized a conservative professor for expecting students "to toe his line in tests" in a course that "reeks of ideological indoctrination." It makes a similar charge against some professors at the other end of the spectrum, saying, "in most classes conducted by liberals, those desirous of a good grade should be well-practised parrots in exams." Of a chemistry professor, *Texas Review* said: "Like most science professors, he thankfully does not burden students with his political views." In short, they—like the *California Review*—see the issue not as one of whose politics you agree with but who takes seriously the responsibility of being a teacher.

Some professors attempt to escape the responsibility of informing students on both sides of issues by saying that "everybody" is biased and that they are simply being more "open" or "honest" about it. In many such cases, the bias is so gross that the professor could not possibly conceal it anyway, so whatever credit he gets (or takes) for openness or honesty is unearned. For example, a history professor at the University of Massachusetts declared: "I am biased. I'm not going to give you both sides to every question." His course "will be consistently anti-American," he said. "This is not a course that is going to make you happy to be an American." This common type of "justification" for indoctrination contains such classic fallacies that it is worth analyzing for a moment.

The purpose of education is not to make you "happy" or unhappy about any subject but to make you *informed*. Deliberate omissions on one side are the antithesis of this. Everyone no doubt has a viewpoint. "Bias" is not simply having a viewpoint but making that viewpoint override other considerations and responsibilities. Sports announcer Frank Gifford may well have a soft spot in his heart for his old football team, the N.Y. Giants. But if his broadcast left out the fact that another team scored a touchdown against the Giants, everyone would consider it outrageous and dishonorable.

Education is at least as important as a football game.

Faculty Scholarship

Although students are able to detect gross neglect or irresponsibility by professors, their general inability to assess professional competence means that direct observation is often inadequate or deceptive. One of the reasons for the "publish or perish" rule for professors is that they need to be forced to demonstrate their understanding of their subject to their peers, who are professionally competent to judge. Liberal arts colleges do not expect their faculty to publish at the frantic pace found in some research universities, but professors at good liberal arts colleges usually publish something—perhaps an undergraduate textbook in their subject, or an occasional article in a scholarly journal. A study cited in the November/December 1986 issue of *Change* magazine showed that the faculty of 48 leading liberal arts colleges published 7,000 journal articles over a five-year period—nearly one-third of them co-authored with students.

Such scholarly activity is not the rule for all professors or at all colleges. Sometimes years—or even decades—can go by without a single sign of scholarly life from a professor, in which case the faculty can easily fall behind the development of their fields. They may be wonderful at teaching what was known or believed 20 years ago—and the students have no way of realizing it. Such obsolescence occurs not only in fast-changing fields like computer science but even in subjects like ancient history, where new archaeological discoveries, old manuscripts unearthed, or new statistical techniques can completely change what was once believed about a whole era of the past.

The shortcomings of undergraduate education at many outstanding research universities might seem to refute the idea that scholarship and good teaching are related. But, like many things that are beneficial in moderation, complete preoccupation with scholarly research can become detrimental to undergraduate education beyond some point. The more basic problem, however, is *not* simply that some great scholars can't or won't teach well.

At many universities, the great scholarly professors are not the ones doing most of the undergraduate teaching in the first place. Often the real problem is one of bait-and-switch education. Harvard does not owe its prestige to its assistant professors or to its graduate students who teach most of its introductory calculus courses. When students are attracted to Harvard by its prestige, they are often likely to be taught by those who had nothing to do with creating it. The classroom shortcomings of those who created the school's research prestige are only part of the problem, and not necessarily the most serious part.

✔ VOCATIONALISM

Colleges not only educate in the classical liberal arts sense, but also prepare students to earn a living after they graduate. Historically, many colleges, including Harvard, began as places to prepare men for careers as religious ministers. Today, the ideal of the liberally educated person is often at war with the practice of preparing people to become engineers, nurses, or accountants.

While education in the liberal arts can accompany training for any profession, the time demands of subjects like engineering may crowd other subjects toward the periphery in terms of the number of courses taken, the time devoted to them, and the interest shown in them. The Carnegie Council makes a formal distinction between the purely liberal arts college and the "comprehensive" college which offers vocational programs (nursing, accounting, teacher training) or pre-professional programs (pre-law, pre-med, pre-business) along with liberal arts programs.

Often, however, vocationalism is a state of mind more than something visible in the curriculum. Even at a purely liberal arts college with no formal pre-med program, the pre-medical student who takes tough courses in biology and chemistry and shops for the easiest courses available in sociology or history to fill out his program has made his own personal choice for vocationalism. This is not essentially different from what happens at a "comprehensive" college when a pre-business student chooses to take all the economics, accounting, and marketing courses available, leaving philosophy and foreign languages for those who want to stop and smell the roses. The absence or near-absence of distribution requirements at many institutions facilitates such pre-professionalism, regardless of whether the institution is labelled "liberal arts" or "comprehensive." That formal distinction seems more misleading than useful and so will not be applied in this book.

Where a college has a fine liberal arts curriculum that all its students take, and take interest in, it is pointless to call it anything other than a liberal arts college, even if it has a program in pre-med or pre-law. From an intellectual standpoint, such programs are usually at least as rigorous as "interdisciplinary" programs that no one seems to think compromises the "liberal arts" designation. However, the distinction between a pervasive pre-professional *atmosphere* on campus and an intellectual, liberal arts atmosphere can be important, even if labels or curriculum alone do not enable you to make an easy formal distinction.

Because of the subjective aspect of pre-professionalism, it is sometimes hard to distinguish the true liberal arts institution from its pre-professional look-alike, where liberal arts subjects are not taken seriously. Nevertheless, the difference is important, even if subjective. If subjects like logic, astronomy, and music excite you, then you are likely to find fewer kindred souls in a college where the "practical" predominates in people's thinking. Indeed, some of the more intellectual subjects may not be taught at all, or not taught by top professors—either because of the college's priorities or because outstanding professors tend to drift away when they sense student disinterest in their field.

If you have little interest in abstract subjects, but want to get on with preparing for a career, a college dedicated to liberal arts in fact as well as in name may have strict distribution requirements that put you through many difficult and time-consuming courses in subjects that have no meaning for you. Sometimes these subjects will acquire meaning, but for some people they never will. The point here is simply that pre-professional vocationalism and an intellectual liberal arts orientation are substantially different, even though they are not formally distinguished in the names of the colleges, except for engineering schools.

Some colleges and universities, at various academic levels, have strong reputations as pre-professional schools (Franklin & Marshall, Simmons, Drexel), while others are known for their intellectual, liberal arts orientations (Chicago, Oberlin, Pomona). Because there are no explicit, formal labels that really distinguish between pre-professional and other liberal arts colleges and universities, these differences have to be checked out college by college, but it is well worth the effort if your own orientation is strongly in one direction or the other. For those who are not sure, there are many colleges and universities that are also not sure.

Some colleges are vocational in more concrete terms. They may be vocational in the sense of having many courses or departments in graphic arts, nursing, journalism, accounting, physical therapy, fashion design, or social work, for example. Where such courses dominate the curriculum, questions may be raised, not only about the quantity but also the quality of the liberal arts courses, because it is hard to have a first-rate liberal arts program where most students are preoccupied with other things. If your own preoccupation is with the vocation you wish to pursue, it may be worth questioning whether you should be pursuing it in a college at all, if there are specialized schools which can provide the same skills as well or better, and without the distraction of liberal arts courses that are watered down.

Those students who are intellectually oriented need not,

of course, abandon all thought of how they will support themselves after graduation. Some majors, such as mathematics, offer promising careers, though others, such as English, usually mean bleak prospects in the job market. However, an English major who has taken some courses in computer science may find it easier to get started on a career.

Many of those with strong intellectual interests in fields such as chemistry, philosophy, or economics will of course continue to pursue those interests in graduate school and go on to become scholars. Others will seek professional degrees in law, business, and other fields—including, if they have taken the right science courses, medicine. No one needs to be pre-law or pre-med to go on to law school or medical school, and some business schools prefer that you not major in business as an undergraduate. Where the chosen career—as economist, philosopher, or chemist, for example—requires graduate training, then the student should feel especially free to use the undergraduate years as a once-in-a-lifetime opportunity to get the broadest and best foundation in liberal arts, in order to be an educated person as well as a professional practitioner.

Those whose formal education will end with college graduation should legitimately be concerned with earning a living the rest of their lives. That doesn't mean that they can't get a liberal arts education but only that it should include something that will help them become self-supporting. The students who get the worst of both worlds are those who get neither an intellectual discipline nor a professional skill from college but instead specialize in some fashionable "interdisciplinary" field like ethnic or women's studies, which leads nowhere intellectually or vocationally, and whose fashion already shows signs of waning.

CHAPTER 6

KINDS OF ENVIRONMENTS

It makes even less sense to try to rank college environments than to try to rank the "top 10" or "top 20" colleges academically. The same social, or even physical, surroundings that make one person happy and productive can weigh like a terrible burden on another. Many people find the Los Angeles climate delightful, but those with respiratory problems can find it distressing or even dangerous, because of the smog. Being far away from home can create a feeling of liberation for some and a feeling of abandonment for others. With environments, even more than with academics, the crucial question is whether there is a match or a mismatch between the individual and the institution.

Things that are environmental are not necessarily incidental. Sometimes they can make or break the whole college experience. Being surrounded by people whose attitudes, values, and beliefs are all radically different from your own can be very trying for four years—or may even make it unlikely that you will last the four years. The physical safety of the environment is also not a trivial consideration—certainly not to someone who has been mugged, raped, or stabbed.

Not all environmental features are negative, of course. On some campuses you may discover an environment richer in every way than anything you have ever known and make friends you will cherish for a lifetime. A whole galaxy of ideas and cultural enlightenment may open up for you.

Colleges differ as much in environments as they do in other ways. Some of these differences, such as in food or in the noise level in the dormitories, can only be checked in person during a campus visit. These are left for Chapter 10. Some other important environmental features to consider in this chapter include (1) location, (2) the sexual environment, and (3) the presence or absence of tolerance for divergent views.

✔ LOCATION

The location of a college matters in a number of ways. If the college is located in or near an urban high-crime area, that obviously matters to everyone. For some, location in an isolated rural setting matters—either positively or negatively. Going to college in a different geograpic region can mean being suddenly surrounded by an entirely different lifestyle, and that in turn can be either refreshing or depressing.

Subtle regional differences in behavior can lead to misunderstandings, even when the people involved are not fundamentally different. For example, people in California are more likely to smile at strangers or to start up conversations with them than people are in the northeast. A young woman from California who goes to college in New York or Boston and goes around smiling at young men and starting up conversations with them may find her intentions misunderstood and her life complicated as a result.

Those who want diversity rather than a different uniformity may be happier in a college that attracts students from around the country, rather than one representing only the culture and values of its own region. Here, certain college guides such as Cass & Birnbaum's *Comparative Guide to American Colleges* can be very useful when they list the geographical origins of some colleges' students. While nationally renowned institutions generally draw students from all over the country and from overseas, this is of course not true of most state colleges and universities. Conversely, there are some institutions that are not nationally renowned which nevertheless have regionally diverse student bodies. The Florida Institute of Technology, for example, has as many students from New England as from the South. As with so many other things, each institution will have to be checked out individually.

How important location is will obviously vary with how adaptable you are. But even those who think of location as incidental may want to reconsider after reflecting on some of the problems connected with distance from home or large differences in climate from what you are used to.

Distance

Distance from home affects more than the psychological impact of going away to college. Distance from home is an important financial factor as well. There is not only the cost of going at the beginning of the academic year and returning at the end, but also all the trips back and forth for Christmas and at other holiday periods or breaks between terms. Staying on campus at such times may not even be possible at some colleges, because they simply close up the dormitories. Even when it is possible to remain on campus, it can be a depressing experience to see a familiar setting suddenly become a ghost town as everyone else heads home.

It may be especially depressing during the freshman year, when so many other problems and adjustments weigh on you. Going home can recharge your batteries. There is a big difference between being alone on a deserted campus and being the center of attention to family and friends at holiday time.

How many breaks in the academic schedule there are depends on the college and how many trips home obviously varies with the individual and the budget. A common pattern, however, would include the trip to college at the beginning of the academic year (one way), trips home for Thanksgiving break (round trip), Christmas break (round trip), Spring break (round trip), and then the return home at the end of the academic year (one way). Even if you don't go beyond this modest schedule, that is still covering the distance between college and home eight times a year. It can matter financially whether that distance represents a couple of hours on a bus or a transcontinental plane ride.

To those who have to keep an eye on the budget, the cost of several trips a year can be very significant. It may be worth a call to an airline or a bus company to find out exactly how much, as one item to consider when choosing a college. The difference between $100 and $300 for a trip from home to colleges at different distances may not seem like much, but when you multiply it by a few trips a year, it can easily add up to a difference of a thousand dollars or more, on top of all the other costs of college.

While the cost of transportation is a factor to keep in mind—which means to write down, if you are serious—it would be a mistake to eliminate any college from consideration at the outset because of its distance. Only after learning specifically what financial aid you will be awarded will you know how much the other costs of college will be

in reality for you. Your own personal costs are what matter, not the numbers printed in catalogues and brochures.
Those numbers are just list prices, in a market where there
are usually large and varying discounts.

Climate

An important feature to check into after you have narrowed your choice of colleges down to a handful is the climate at each of the places remaining on your short list.
Someone from Florida who leaves home for the first time
to go to college in Minnesota may be in for quite a shock
from the weather, on top of all the other changes and
stresses that plague the freshman year. Even aside from
temperature differences, some people from sunny climates
may become depressed in places where leaden, overcast
skies prevail for weeks on end. If you are thinking about
Cornell University or the University of Michigan, this kind
of weather is a fact of life to consider, along with heavy
snowfalls. Seattle has a relatively mild climate the year
around—but it receives only about half the sunshine of
Phoenix, Arizona.

When considering colleges a long way from home, it
would be a mistake to assume that they have similar climates when they are in the same state. On the Pacific coast,
especially, there may be very large variations in weather
within a few miles. In Los Angeles, it is not uncommon for
coastal areas to have summertime temperatures in the 60s
while downtown L.A. has temperatures in the 90s—and
parts of the city located in the San Fernando Valley may
hit 100 at the same time. Colleges located in the coastal
regions of southern California in general have not only significantly different temperature patterns from inland colleges but also very different amounts of fresh air and smog.

Pepperdine University is only about 50 miles from Whittier College, but Pepperdine is on a hill overlooking Malibu Beach and gets fresh ocean breezes, while Whittier is out in the smoggy area north of Disneyland. Anyone with respiratory problems would be well advised to consult a physician before considering any of the colleges in the eastern part of the Los Angeles basin, even though there are many fine academic institutions in that area, including Cal Tech and the whole Claremont group of colleges.

In Washington state and Oregon, coastal areas differ from inland areas somewhat in temperature but much more so in rainfall. The University of Washington in Seattle gets *several times* the rainfall of Whitman College, located further inland in the same state. While visiting the University of Puget Sound on a bright sunny day, I noticed that the local residents spoke of the weather as an almost miraculous event. The University of Puget Sound is located in Tacoma, not far from Seattle, and gets the heavy rainfall and lingering overcasts typical of the Washington and Oregon coasts.

If rainfall doesn't bother you but bitter cold does, then the coastal Pacific Northwest may be an attractive area. Although Seattle is much farther north than Washington, D.C., winter temperatures are virtually the same in the two cities. Seattle is one degree warmer in January and three degrees warmer in February. Both cities have significantly milder winters than New England, the Great Lakes region, or the Northern Plains states.

Except for people with health problems, or people whose moods are seriously affected by gloomy weather or bitter cold, or devotees of tennis or skiing, it probably isn't worth going very deeply into the climate patterns at various colleges until the number of institutions has been reduced to perhaps half a dozen that you are pretty sure you want to apply to. Then it may be worthwhile to start getting some very specific hard facts. Monthly temperature charts for various cities are available in the state-by-state "TourBooks" which the American Automobile Association provides free to its members. If you are not a member of AAA, you may want to write to the respective Chambers of Commerce in the communities where the colleges are located to ask for climate information. If you want to get into detail on things like rainfall, snowfall, and sunshine, the U.S. Bureau of the Census publishes a *Climatic Atlas of the United States*, which will tell you all you want to know, and more.

Campus visits are of very limited use as regards climate, since all you can see is the weather on the particular days when you happen to be there. In extreme cases, however—someone from the sun belt thinking of going to a college in the snow belt—it may be very useful for an Alabama or Arizona student to visit Carleton College in Minnesota or Middlebury College in Vermont in January, to see how it feels to be in freezing weather, or perhaps a blizzard. Conversely, someone from Massachusetts visiting the University of San Diego in January may decide, after a day at the beach, that it is too pleasant to pass up.

✔ THE SEXUAL ENVIRONMENT

Sexual issues do not exist in isolation but affect the whole social atmosphere of a campus The ease with which you can make friends, and the unspoken expectations surrounding these friendships, can be affected by whether the individual has been matched or mismatched with the college, in terms of values and attitudes. A girl who says "no" can find herself isolated on a campus where virtually all the other girls say "yes." Conversely, a girl who says "yes" can become an outcast on a campus where almost all the other girls say "no." Either situation can be especially painful at a small college, where everybody knows everybody else—and everybody else's business.

The policies, practices, and attitudes of colleges and their officials can influence the social environment, which can be of enormous importance to the personal as well as academic development of a student. The question is not whether the college's sexual restrictions (if any) are 100 percent effective against those determined to violate them, or whether students with traditional values will all succumb to campus permissiveness and peer pressure. There is a vast spectrum between these extremes, and the attitudes and expectations of a college, as well as its explicit policies, can influence where many students end up on that spectrum.

The Avant-Garde

Because attitudes and official policies on sexual questions are often radically different from what they were just 20 years ago, parents especially need to understand that their college memories may bear *no resemblance whatever* to the reality on some campuses today. For example, among the materials routinely handed out during registration at Dartmouth College is a "safer sex kit," described in its own literature as being "for everyone—homosexual, bisexual, and heterosexual." Included in the kit are devices for use in these various kinds of activity. After noting in passing that "abstinence is always an option," the literature urges the student to "be imaginative and creative" in sexual matters. Suggestions are offered.

Parental influence is finessed out of the picture early on in the principal booklet accompanying Dartmouth's "safer sex kit." According to the booklet, sex "is too important a personal decision" to let "someone else" decide, though you may "clarify your thinking by talking to friends." While parents are not included among those who have any clarification to offer, they are included among a list of people to turn to after a shattered "relationship" has turned out to be emotionally "devastating." In short, the parent's role is to help pick up the pieces afterward.

As with so many other aspects of choosing a college, it is necessary for parents and students to be clear in their own minds as to what they do and do not want, and to find out what the specifics are at any particular college being considered. This is especially so in this controversial area, where official policy is often camouflaged by words, to avoid the wrath of parents. "Intervisitation unlimited" is one of those cryptic phrases that parents may pass over as just more dull academic jargon—unless they realize that it means the college does nothing to discourage men from spending the night in bed with their daughter.

"Sex education" is another phrase that often means far more than the words say. In colleges, as in so many other settings, "sex education" is *not* simply a matter of making certain biological or medical information available to students. It is the active promotion of a whole set of attitudes, beliefs, and values, often radically different from those acquired at home, and in one way or another presented as superior, more sophisticated, and more modern than what was taught by parents or by "society." This may or may not coincide with your views, either on sex or on the role of a college. Whatever your views, you need to understand that this is often the concrete reality behind the bland words, "sex education"—and that your decision is about this reality, not about what the words alone might suggest.

Although Dartmouth is among those in the vanguard of the sexual revolution on campus, it is by no means unique in using routine biological information—much of it already known in essence by the students—as a vehicle for transmitting new "sexual styles" and attitudes. Stanford's "sex education" material is even more plainly an incitement rather than a mere set of biological information. It includes a booklet entitled "SAFE SEX EXPLORER'S ACTION PACKED STARTER KIT HANDBOOK," which begins: "WELCOME EXPLORERS! THIS IS THE SAFE SEX UNIVERSE where you will find MANY NEW GALAXIES OF HOT & HEALTHY RISK REDUCTION, PLEASURE *and* PEACE OF MIND!!" It urges: "Take time for yourself each day specifically devoted to safe sex." Clinical language is in several places discarded for four-letter words as they offer suggestions for a wide variety of sexual practices, both homosexual and heterosexual. Even more devices are included for use in these various practices than are included in Dartmouth's kit.

At the University of Puget Sound, a full-page ad in the student newspaper shows two cartoon individuals with little hearts scattered around them and these words:

> When it came to safe sex, I thought he'd be like all the rest . . . quick, boring and then long gone. How could I have *known* he had been to the workshop? How could I have *known* he was about to give me the most searingly romantic night of my life? And how could I have known he would want to *stay*? He gave me . . . "A dozen red condoms."

Just how cute this is obviously depends on your viewpoint and your values. Clearly, however, it is a work of advocacy rather than information.

Some sex education material at some institutions is in fact a sober, straightforward presentation of biological and medical information. The University of Connecticut, for example, provides this kind of sex education literature. However, the specifics must be determined by finding out just what "sex education" means at each institution.

Whether the incitement factor outweighs whatever medical information accompanies it in "sex education" material is a judgment that must be weighed by each individual. It should *not* be assumed, for example, that such material reduces the risk of pregnancy on net balance. Stanford alone averages more than a hundred unwanted pregnancies a year—and it is by no means unique.

On some campuses, homosexuality is a much larger phenomenon than many parents or students might imagine. It is not simply a question of there being some individuals of this sort but of organized, vocal gay and lesbian organizations, whose promotion of their particular lifestyle has the active backing of the college authorities, who can be swift in their punishment of other students who express any criticism. If that seems hard to believe, some illustrations may be in order.

An article in *The Wall Street Journal* by the wife of a Yale University faculty member suggested that about one-fourth of Yale students were homosexuals. Though the figure was disputed, the influence of homosexuals at Yale cannot be. When their posters around campus for "gay awareness" were parodied by other posters put out by another student, that student was suspended for two years by the Yale administration—and warned that anything like that again would result in his permanent expulsion. The dean of Yale's own law school protested against the way the student was treated. Even violence on campus is seldom met with such severe punishment.

This episode was not unique. It symbolized the influence of an organized and vocal group which exists on a number of campuses, and which many parents and students may be wholly unaware of before choosing a college. At the University of Massachusetts, a student was threatened with expulsion merely for removing a poster put on a bulletin board by a homosexual organization. At Harvard, a student was suspended for removing a sign from a lunchroom table showing that that table was reserved for a gay and lesbian organization.

On some campuses where any criticism of homosexuality brings condemnation of the critic as showing "homophobia" (sometimes punishable in the same way as racism), promotion of homosexuality is quite permissible, as in an advertisement in Dartmouth's student newspaper with this heading: "IF YOU'VE NEVER SLEPT WITH A PERSON OF THE SAME SEX, IS IT POSSIBLE THAT ALL YOU NEED IS A GOOD GAY LOVER?"

Those who are avant-garde may be cheered by such developments and those who are traditional may be appalled. Both need to be aware of such recent trends—and aware also of how the particular colleges they are considering do or do not participate in these trends.

The Traditional

Sexual policies vary as widely as all other policies at colleges and universities. There are institutions where most—or all—students live in single-sex dormitories, where attitudes and practices remain traditional, and where there are no homosexual organizations nor any known homosexuals. Often, there are schools which reflect traditional values in other ways as well. However, these are by no means all Bible Belt fundamentalist colleges. Institutions where less than half the women students live in co-ed dorms, and where male visitors cannot stay overnight in their rooms, stretch from coast to coast and cover an academic range that includes colleges whose students' average S.A.T. scores go from below the national average of about 900 to above 1200. Some have more than 7 percent of their graduates continue on to receive Ph.D.'s, which is to say that they are among the top 70 institutions in the country (out of about 3,000) in that regard.

While co-ed dormitories are a symbol of sharp policy changes by colleges during the current generation, the question is not simply whether there are co-ed dorms. The question is also what percentage of the students live in them, and under what rules—if any. Intervisitation policy is at least as important as co-ed dorms, and the two policies do not always go together. For example, Randolph-Macon College in Virginia has no co-ed dorms but allows unlimited visitations in rooms of the opposite sex, except where the students in particular dorms vote limitations of their own. Conversely, Santa Clara University in California has co-ed dorms (with men and women on separate floors) but prohibits overnight stays in rooms belonging to members of the opposite sex. Single-sex dorms at single-sex colleges likewise have intervisitation policies which range from some restricted weekend hours for male visitors at Agnes Scott College in Georgia to permitting overnight boy friends at Mills College in California. The only real restriction at Mills seems to be "in no case may an overnight guest stay for more than four consecutive nights."

Because co-ed dorms and unlimited visitation have become so widespread, those who are seeking either or both should have no problem finding them. College guides sometimes include such information in their descriptions of particular institutions but the brochures issued by the colleges themselves may avoid the subject entirely, for fear of arousing parental concerns. In any event, the sheer number of colleges and universities with co-ed dorms and/or unlimited visitation is far too large for them to be listed here.

The more difficult problem is for those parents and students who are seeking a more traditional kind of atmosphere. Not only must they search more; they may even be led to believe that "everybody" has co-ed dorms and unlimited access to the opposite sex. That is simply not true. Even in avant-garde California, Pepperdine University has no co-ed dorms and has a very restrictive policy on visits with the opposite sex, as well as a complete prohibition on alcohol. Pepperdine's undergraduates have very respectable academic credentials, and its business school is ranked among the best in the region.

Even in these enlightened and liberated times, still only women get pregnant. Parents of young women may therefore be especially concerned about the sexual atmosphere on campus. Moreover, some parents may not consider an all-female college a desirable alternative on various grounds, including militant lesbianism at some women's institutions, such as Smith College or Wellesley.

The following is a *partial* list of 50 co-educational colleges and universities where (1) less than half the women live in co-ed dorms, where (2) there are limitations of one sort or another on male visitors, and where (3) the average S.A.T. or A.C.T. test score equals or exceeds the national average:

College	% of Women in Co-ed Dorms	Location	Composite Score	
Assumption College	0	Worcester, MA 01609	S.A.T.	936
Auburn University	0	Auburn Univ., AL 36849-5425	S.A.T.	1067
Augustana College	2	Rock Island, IL 61201	A.C.T.	24.4
Austin College	28	Sherman, TX 75090	S.A.T.	1046
Baldwin-Wallace College	0	Berea, OH 44017	S.A.T.	927
Baylor University	0	Waco, TX 76798	S.A.T.	1039
Benedictine College	0	Atchison, KS 66002	A.C.T.	21
Berea College	0	Berea, KY 40403	S.A.T.	910
Berry College	0	Mount Berry, GA 30149	S.A.T.	979
Birmingham-Southern College*	0	Birmingham, AL 35204	A.C.T.	24.5
Briar Cliff College	33	Sioux City, IA 51104	A.C.T.	20.8
Calvin College	0	Grand Rapids, MI 49506	S.A.T.	1049
Canisius College	0	Buffalo, NY 14108	S.A.T.	1024
Catholic University*	15	Washington, DC 20064	S.A.T.	1050
Centenary College	0	Shreveport, LA 71134-1188	S.A.T.	1007
Coe College	16	Cedar Rapids, IA 52402	A.C.T.	23
Concordia College	0	Moorehead, MN 56560	A.C.T.	23
Davidson College*	31	Davidson, NC 28036	S.A.T.	1220
Furman University	0	Greenville, SC 29613	S.A.T.	1118
Grove City College	0	Grove City, PA 16127	S.A.T.	1066
Guilford College	10	Greensboro, NC 27410	S.A.T.	985
Hastings College	0	Hastings, NE 68901	A.C.T.	21
Hendrix College	18	Conway, Arkansas 72032	S.A.T.	1099
Hillsdale College	0	Hillsdale, MI 49242	S.A.T.	945

Institution		Address	Test	Score
Hope College*	30	Holland, MI 49423	S.A.T.	1050
Houghton College	0	Houghton, NY 14744	S.A.T.	1068
Illinois Wesleyan University	14	Bloomington, IL 61701	A.C.T.	24.6
Miami University	15	Oxford, OH 45056	S.A.T.	1100
Millikin University	17	Decatur, IL 62522	A.C.T.	23.5
Millsaps College	5	Jackson, MS 39202	S.A.T.	1100
Moravian College	4	Bethlehem, PA 18018	S.A.T.	1016
Mount Union College	0	Alliance, OH 44601	S.A.T.	928
Otterbein College	4	Westerville, OH 43081	S.A.T.	932
Pepperdine University	0	Malibu, CA 90265	S.A.T.	1072
Rhodes College*	0	Memphis, TN 38112	S.A.T.	1157
Ripon College	17	Ripon, WI 54971	S.A.T.	1039
Rockford College	18	Rockford, IL 61108	S.A.T.	980
Stetson University	0	DeLand, FL 3270-3757	S.A.T.	1084
St. Norbert College	18	DePere, WI 54115	A.C.T.	22.5
Trinity University	30	San Antonio, TX 78284	S.A.T.	1205
University of Dallas	0	Irving, TX 75062	S.A.T.	1185
University of Dayton	0	Dayton, OH 45469	S.A.T.	992
University of Notre Dame	0	Notre Dame, IN 46556	S.A.T.	1198
University of Portland	0	Portland, OR 97203	S.A.T.	964
University of Richmond	0	Richmond, VA 23173	S.A.T.	1155
Ursinus College	16	Collegeville, PA 19426	S.A.T.	1095
Villanova University	0	Villanova, PA 19085	S.A.T.	1114
Wake Forest University	30	Winston-Salem, NC 27109	S.A.T.	1140
Wheaton College* (Illinois)	0	Wheaton, IL 60187	S.A.T.	1126
Wofford College	0	Spartanburg, SC 29301	S.A.T.	1041

*More than 7 percent of graduates go on to the Ph.D.

This list, like other lists, is meant to be suggestive and a helpful starting point for your own investigation. It is not meant to be the last word. Certainly it does not mean that every college on this list will meet all the desires of those who want traditional living arrangements, not to mention other academic or environmental requirements. Nor does it mean that students in all other colleges left off the list have unlimited access to the opposite sex.

Purdue University, for example, is not on this list because its on-campus students are split evenly between single-sex dormitories and co-ed dormitories. However, it does not permit overnight visits with the opposite sex. Conversely, Davidson College is on the list but about half of all "sexually active" students there have the sexually transmitted chlamydia bacterium, according to the college physician. What percentage of Davidson students are in fact "sexually active" was not disclosed. Washington State University in Pullman, Washington, was eligible for the list, since it has more women in single-sex dorms than in co-ed dorms and limits intervisitation. But it was not included because its intervisitation limit is 2 A.M. Obviously, these were judgment calls and the list could have been expanded or contracted by different judgments. In short, there is not a hard and fast line between traditional and other living arrangements. One shades off into the other. The 50 institutions listed are meant to show that rules do apply in many institutions and to suggest some to look at, if you are concerned about such things.

Campus visits are perhaps the best way to assess the situation as regards sexual policies and practices at a given college — especially if a student visitor stays in a dormitory overnight and can talk to other students there without parents or officials around. Parents can also get some information by asking frank questions in the admissions office and at the dean of students office (they may or may not say the same thing).

For those who do not make campus visits, questions may be asked of college representatives when they visit your high school. Telephone calls to the college campus may get information directly or through the mail. If the college has "sex education" material, ask to see it, offer to pay for it, including whatever kits may be supplied. If people you know are going to college there, ask them or their parents.

Two very different written sources of information on this subject may also prove useful to you: (1) Lisa Birnbach, chic and trendy author, and (2) conservative student newspapers at various colleges. *Lisa Birnbach's College Book* includes dating, sex, and the "gay situation" among the things she comments on in her descriptions of various institutions. Whether or not you share her breezy approach to some of these issues, she offers more of this kind of information and assessments than other college guides. Similarly, conservative student newspapers can be a useful source of information, whether you share their political views or not. Where there is a separate conservative student newspaper on campus, in addition to the official student newspaper, the writers on the more conservative paper tend to comment adversely from time to time on the sexual revolution on campus in general or homosexuals in particular. Whether or not you agree with their comments, you are more likely to get information from this quarter than from others who simply take for granted whatever the sexual attitudes and practices happen to be.

✔ TOLERATION

One of the things that makes a campus environment not only pleasant or unpleasant but also stimulating or stifling to your general development is the degree of toleration there. Like everything else, this varies enormously from college to college. They differ not only in how much toleration there is but also—and perhaps more importantly—in the particular things that are tolerated and not tolerated.

Yale's toleration of pro-homosexual posters obviously did not extend to toleration of anti-homosexual posters. At Dartmouth, pro-divestment demonstrators repeatedly violated campus rules and local laws with their disruptions, without being punished, but the first anti-divestment disruption was met with swift and lengthy suspensions of the students involved.

On various campuses around the country, virtually nothing promoting the "sexual revolution" is considered too disgusting to be permitted (including pornographic slides in class at Arizona State, a lecturer at Stanford advocating adults having sex with children, or classroom movies at San Francisco State showing humans having sex with animals), but an anti-abortion poster showing dead fetuses was banned at Oregon State as not showing "good taste."

Radical environmentalist Barry Commoner has no trouble giving a speech at Berkeley but Ambassador Jeane Kirkpatrick heads a long list of other speakers who have been unable to talk there because of disruptions. Similar censorship-by-disruption has occurred at colleges across the country over the past several years—at Harvard, Wellesley, Northwestern, Georgetown, and the universities of Massachusetts, Wisconsin, and Colorado, among other places.

Not only students but even faculty members have taken part in disruptions and assaults on speakers, usually with impunity from both the law and from university punishment. A number of nationwide campus organizations have openly asserted that they will disrupt speakers whose opinions they find offensive. A faculty member affiliated with such an organization stormed onto the stage at Northwestern, seized the microphone from the speaker and declared: "He has no right to speak . . . He'll be lucky to get out of here alive." The speaker was in fact taken away as a protective precaution against the swarm of disrupters who had stormed on stage.

A series of similar assaults at Harvard have prevented speakers from being heard there and threatened their physical safety. Despite calls for punishment of disrupters by both the liberal *Harvard Crimson* and the conservative *Harvard Salient*, the college's Dean of the Faculty said: "We rely on basic human decency as the ultimate corrective mechanism to insure freedom of speech." Such tolerance of intolerance is not peculiar to Harvard, nor is the lofty rhetoric that he used to cover capitulation.

Refusal to prosecute assaults or to administer academic punishment to disrupters is the key to continuing censorship-by-disruption on campuses across the country. In turn, this means that speakers likely to offend the disruptive elements are less likely to be invited—and less likely to accept, if they are.

What does this have to do with choosing a college? Just as you cannot know what you were *not* taught in a course, so you cannot know what you have not heard elsewhere on campus. On economic, political, and social issues, you need to hear a range of views for your own intellectual development, whether or not your opinion is changed.

Stifling speakers means cheating you. On campuses where social science courses reflect a narrow range of views by ideologically committed professors, stopping outsiders from showing you other perspectives can mean cheapening your education. In this particular era, the political left has done the stifling. In other times and places, other political forces have done so. Educationally, it is all the same—and it is all negative.

What needs to be checked out about any college you are considering is not whether its politics are left or right, but whether there is honesty and diversity in the classrooms and on the campus. Find out who is invited to lecture on campus. If it is a steady diet of one viewpoint, that tells you something—no matter what that viewpoint is.

Intolerance on some campuses extends right into the classroom. At Kenyon College, during a campaign for radical feminism, women who went to class dressed in traditional fashion were subjected to embarrassment by students and faculty alike. At the University of Michigan, a student had her grade reduced in an English class because she used the word "Congressman" instead of her teacher's ideological preference, "Congressperson." At Howard University, a student who had written an editorial in the college newspaper, defending the landing of American troops in Grenada, was sitting quietly in class when he heard the professor refer to him as a "fascist." At Stanford, a young woman who wrote an essay in the student newspaper criticizing a statement by a Marxist professor later heard her essay denounced from the lecture platform by that professor in a stream of obscenities.

All too many put-downs of students for ideological reasons occur on other campuses. This is something to check out during a campus visit by talking to students. It is hard to know how else to discover such things, unless you happen to be sitting in on a class when it happens. If you are, be sure to ask students how common it is. Write down their answers in a notebook that you can go back to later, when it is time to choose a college.

Social life and even employment opportunities can be affected by intolerance on campus. Where many students are convinced that there is only one way to look at certain issues, anyone who sees it differently, or who simply refuses to take sides at all, can find it harder to make friends than those who go along wholeheartedly with whatever the prevailing belief happens to be.

Even your opportunities for summer jobs or future careers can be reduced on campuses with organized disruptions of recruiters for private companies or government agencies that are out of political favor with the student activists. Such employers may not be invited in by the college authorities in order to avoid unpleasant scenes, or may not choose to come themselves if a needless hassle is likely. Whatever the immediate target of campus intolerance, the real loser may be you, not only intellectually and socially but in financial and career terms as well.

CHAPTER 7

MINORITY STUDENTS

The term "minority" is used in a special sense by most colleges. Black, Hispanic, American Indian, and sometimes Asian American students are included, but certainly not Jewish or Irish students. It is not a statistical concept.

When the University of California at Berkeley established a minimum cut-off score on the verbal S.A.T. for admission, it exempted "minority" students—but not Asian Americans. When the U.S. Air Force Academy established lower cut-off scores for minority students, it technically included Asians as minorities but assigned them the same cut-off scores as for whites. Yet when counting how many minority students have been admitted, most colleges count Asian Americans, even if Asian Americans have received no special help in admissions—or even if there were special barriers against them, as seems to be the case in some places.

In short, the term "minority" as used by most colleges has no clear-cut definition, no consistent principle, and no coherent theory behind it. Minority students are whomever they choose to consider minority students. In practice, the term usually refers to whatever racial or ethnic groups have a statistical "representation" the colleges wish to increase beyond what it would be if the usual admission standards were applied. Blacks are the prime example, but much of what is said about blacks applies as well to Hispanics and American Indians.

In this chapter the main focus will be on black students, simply because more information is available on them. However, there will also be a separate discussion of Asian American students, because they are often treated differently from either blacks or whites by the colleges themselves.

✔ BLACK STUDENTS

When black students go to black colleges, it is much like white students going to white colleges, in terms of the kinds of things to look for when making your choices. The more challenging problem comes when black students go to colleges that are predominantly white, sometimes overwhelmingly white. Because such colleges are by far the most numerous, and are spread out over a wider range of social, geographic, and academic diversity, these will be the main focus here.

"The races in the Northern universities have grown more separate since the sixties," according to Professor Allan Bloom in his best-selling book, *The Closing of the American Mind*. He is not the only one to notice this disturbing phenomenon. The Dean of Students at Middlebury College reported that—for the first time in her long career—some white freshmen in 1986 asked not to be

assigned a black roommate. So did some white freshmen
entering in 1987. Racist graffiti and even physical assaults
against black students occur on campuses where neither
occurred 20 or 30 years ago. In 1987, a black student at
Harvard suffered a smashed window and harassing, racist
phone calls from white students. The first black student
graduated from Harvard more than a hundred years ago,
and a black student was elected class marshall more than
30 years ago by the class of 1958.

The reasons for this retrogression are a matter of controversy. But the important thing for minority students
and their parents to understand is that it is a fact. Minority
parents with good memories of their own college experience
on predominantly white campuses should not automatically
assume that their children can find a similar environment
on the same campuses today.

Fortunately, the negative trends are not universal.
There are campuses where no such retrogression has taken
place over the past generation, and some on which im-
proved relations among the races have occurred. This
means that black parents and students have an extra set
of considerations to check out when choosing a college. It
also means that this extra investment of time and effort is
very much worth making.

Something as intangible as the racial atmosphere on a
campus is not as likely to be known to high school counselors, nor do most college guides go into the subject very
much, if at all. Moreover, what would constitute a "good"
racial environment differs radically between one black student and another. For example, some black students at
Stanford University consider it beneficial that there are
special living quarters where black students are concentrated, while other black students dislike the idea and

resent any pressures to get them to move into these en-
claves. Similarly sharp differences of opinion are found
among Asian, Hispanic, and American Indian students.

If you are a black student looking for a campus where
your academic and social life involves people from all races,
including foreign students, then you may not be happy on
a campus where black students continually group together,
especially if you get negative reactions from fellow blacks
whenever you have lunch or go to a movie with someone
who isn't black. But, if what you are looking for is a campus
where black students do stick together, for mutual support
and for concerted action on campus to achieve their special
goals, then you may be happy at the same college where
the more "integrationist" black student is uncomfortable or
even miserable. The important practical question here is
not which position is "right" but which position is *you*. Talking this over with parents before choosing a college is a
good way to help think through your priorities, especially
if you and your parents have different views and talk them
out.

If you are seeking a campus where black students form
a separate community, then Cornell, Dartmouth, Wesleyan, and Davidson are among many that have that kind
of environment. But if you are seeking a campus where
black students interact socially as individuals in the larger
campus community, then you may want to investigate
places like Haverford, Whitman, George Mason University, the University of San Diego, or the University of
Puget Sound.

Related to the question of the college racial environment
is the question of how you plan to spend your time in college. On many predominantly white campuses there are
Black Studies departments, Black Student Unions, and

often campus political activity related to either or both. Aside from whether you agree or disagree with the goals or methods of this activity, there is the question of how much time you are prepared to devote to activism of any sort.

There are other aspects of budgeting time to think about. In *The Black Student's Guide to Colleges*, there is a recurring emphasis on the number and nature of parties on campus. For example, a black student at Princeton is quoted: "Parties are not given often enough, and when they are, they just don't jump!" Again, it is necessary to be clear in your own mind as to what you are and are not looking for. (My own reaction to the Princeton comment was to recall a scene from an old war-movie melodrama called "The Guns of Navarone." When the Allied commandos had completed their mission and were getting ready to return from behind enemy lines, someone noticed that one of their members was missing. His partner knew that the missing man had gotten into a needless shoot-out with some Nazis and had been killed. "He forgot why we came here," his partner said.)

Despite its emphasis on parties, athletics, campus politics, and other extra-curricular activities, *The Black Student's Guide to Colleges* may be worth looking at simply because it is "the only game in town" as a black student's college guide. It must be read very judiciously, however, because it lacks any depth or judiciousness of its own.

The Mismatching Problem

A common theme of *The Black Student's Guide to Colleges*, and of some other guides, is the need of minority students for special remedial education in college. The grossly inadequate education provided by many ghetto high schools is part of the reason—but only part. Given the vast range of academic standards in American colleges and universities, anyone who is capable of filling out an application form is capable of meeting the normal academic standards of some institutions, somewhere in the system. Given the wide range of academic capabilities among black students, there is no inherent reason why they could not distribute themselves among the corresponding levels of colleges, just as white students tend to do.

In reality, this is not what usually happens. Minority students are systematically *mismatched* with institutions. It starts at the top colleges and universities, whose visibility and prestige make it politically necessary that they have a significant "representation" of blacks among their students. The wealth of such institutions enables them to offer the large-scale financial aid that many black students need to attend any college.

The drive to get a good-looking "body count" of black students leads the top colleges and universities to go way beyond the pool of black students who meet their normal admission standards. For example, there are numerous universities, liberal arts colleges, and technical institutes whose students' combined S.A.T. scores average 1200 or above. Yet a recent study indicated that less than 600 black students in the entire country score this high annually. That would not be enough to supply the Ivy League alone with a good statistical "representation" of black students who meet their normal standards.

Under these conditions, many black students discover too late that the "opportunity" to go to a big-name school turns out to be a trap. It is not a question whether black students are "qualified" but whether they are *mismatched*. For example, the average black student at the Massachusetts Institute of Technology has a higher S.A.T. score in math than 90 percent of all American students. These black students can hardly be considered "unqualified." But, although these students' scores are in the top 10 percent among Americans in general, their scores are in the *bottom* 10 percent among the extraordinary students at M.I.T. Despite much lofty talk about the "irrelevance" of test scores, mismatching of this magnitude does have its effects. More than one-fourth of the black students fail to graduate at M.I.T., and those who do have significantly lower grades than the other students.

This is a needless disaster among highly capable individuals. There are numerous engineering schools at which they could have succeeded, or even excelled. Many individuals with all the ingredients of success have been artificially turned into failures by being *mismatched* with M.I.T. This is not a situation peculiar to this institution. It is an all too common experience for minority students throughout American higher education.

Twenty years ago, I discovered the same phenomenon at Cornell University. With half the black students there on academic probation, despite being steered to easier courses, I became concerned as to what the reason could be and looked up their records. The average black student at Cornell at that time scored at the 75th percentile on the S.A.T. test—that is, was academically superior to three-quarters of all American students. These were not "unqualified" students. But the average white student with whom they were competing in the liberal arts college was at the 99th percentile. Blacks with the qualifications for success were artificially turned into failures by being mismatched with Cornell.

More recently, the same phenomenon has been reported

at the University of California at Berkeley. Although black students at Berkeley have S.A.T. scores slightly above the national average, nearly three-quarters of them fail to graduate. This is a devastating loss of capable young people. Moreover, it is getting worse. Fewer blacks graduated from Berkeley in 1986 than in 1975, even though the total number of black students at Berkeley in 1986 was significantly larger. More are just not making it through.

When choosing a college, you don't want to become one of these statistics. The big-name college's problem is how to get "enough" black students on campus so that the college looks good. Your problem is how to get a good education. No bigger mistake could be made, by students of any race, than to assume that you get a better education at a more prestigious college. For any given individual, the education may be much worse.

When one course alone assigns hundreds of pages of reading per week, those students without the necessary reading speed are going to fall further and further behind, understanding less and less of what is said in class. That's not a better education. When mathematical material that would normally take three semesters to cover is covered in two semesters at a school whose students average 700 on math S.A.T.'s, that is not a better education for people whose math background is not at that stratospheric level. They may have no idea what anybody is talking about, halfway through the first semester, even if they are perfectly capable of learning the same material when taught at a normal pace elsewhere.

Fast-paced courses skimp on explanations and assume that you either have a solid math background or can fill in the gaps on your own. For students with extraordinary math scores, that is probably a reasonable assumption—but not for anybody else.

Because mathematics is an important ingredient in other fields (engineering, economics, chemistry, etc.), a failure to master math can eliminate your opportunity to major in a number of other disciplines. You may enter a prestigious college or university planning to become an economist or an engineer, and end up being forced to major in some other field with less math, less interest, and less prospect of a career. This is especially likely to happen at some large research university where the foundation courses in math are taught by disinterested graduate students, some speaking heavily accented English that is difficult to understand. Your chances of having the full range of choices open to you may well be better at a smaller institution where you are taught by professors specializing in teaching and where the other students have math capabilities similar to yours.

The mismatching of students to colleges is not confined to the top institutions, but is common across a broad spectrum. When the top-level schools recruit black students who would normally be qualified to succeed at the level next to the top, then the second tier of institutions faces the prospect of either (1) being conspicuously lacking in minority students or (2) dipping down to the next level below to bring in enough minority students for a statistically respectable "representation." Usually they end up mismatching students. Once begun at the top, this process continues on down the line.

Test Scores

Soberly comparing your S.A.T. or other test scores with those of the students you would be competing with at a particular college is one way to avoid getting mismatched academically. You may be told that test scores don't really matter because they are "culturally biased" against minority students. Unfortunately, life is "culturally biased" as well. Whatever you achieve or fail to achieve will be in some particular culture.

If the "cultural bias" argument means that a minority student with math and verbal S.A.T. scores in the 400s each is likely to match the academic performance of other students whose math and verbal S.A.T.'s are in the 600s, then this is a dangerous falsehood—one that has ruined the academic chances (and life chances) of vast numbers of minority students, not only at M.I.T., Cornell, and Berkeley, but also at other institutions that keep such politically explosive data under lock and key.

Many people have their own reasons for saying that test scores underestimate the future academic performance of minority or disadvantaged students. But the factual evidence *against* this widespread belief is overwhelming. Anyone seriously interested in the facts is urged to read *Choosing Elites* by Robert Klitgaard, though this is just one of many factual studies with the same result, covering a variety of tests, and extending internationally. The cold fact is that, on average, minority students with low scores perform no better in college than majority students with low scores. This is not peculiar to blacks and whites, or to disadvantaged Americans compared to Americans in general. The same pattern exists in other countries as well.

In the Philippines, for example, people living in Manila tend to score higher on tests than people living in the hinterlands. This may well be due to cultural differences rather than because people in Manila are born any smarter. But the bottom line is that low-scoring people from the hinterlands do not do any better in college than low-scoring people from Manila. It is the same story in Indonesia, where people from the island of Java score higher than people in the outer islands. But low-scoring people from the outer islands do not perform any better at the university than low-scoring people from Java. When the same pattern is found in the United States, it is often vehemently denied by substituting rhetoric for evidence.

One of the reasons why this issue arouses such emotional attacks on test scores is that many people confuse this issue with various attempts to label blacks or other minority groups as being genetically inferior mentally. When black orphans raised by white families average the same I.Q. scores as whites, it seems to me pretty clear that racial differences in test scores are a cultural phenomenon. But cultural disadvantages are very real and very serious in their effects. From a practical standpoint, it doesn't matter how you got your disadvantage; it is still a disadvantage. Natural intelligence is not a complete substitute for a good education, good study habits, and wide cultural experience. It is wishful thinking to believe that it is.

Closing the Gap

Many middle-class white families begin training their children's minds when they are still in the crib. Educational toys for babies and toddlers are followed by books, magazines, and encyclopedias as they grow up, often followed by sending them to summer camps that offer courses on computers or other subjects. After 18 years of this, the differences between advantaged and disadvantaged students can be enormous. That doesn't mean that the disadvantaged student should give up. It does mean that the bitter facts about this disparity must be faced before it is possible to do something about it.

Many minority students and their parents will be

shocked to discover how far behind their educational level is, compared to the level reached by other students with whom they will be competing in college. For example, in 1987 only three high schools in the entire city of Chicago scored as high as the national average on the A.C.T. college entrance examination—and 33 Chicago high schools scored in the bottom 1 percent by national norms. Students from schools like this have enormous amounts of ground to make up, just to compete with the average American student, much less with those students educated in the top public and private high schools.

If your S.A.T. scores are too low for any of the colleges discussed so far, you need not abandon hope. Not only are there colleges whose average S.A.T. levels will match yours; there are also ways to beef up your academic skills before going to college, which will probably raise your scores as well. If you are very serious about going to a college with high academic standards and are willing to do whatever it takes to prepare for such a place, then a year of hard study between high school and college may bring you up to the level you want. There are many ways of doing this—and of financing it.

Spending a year at a community college boning up on basics in math and English will do the job for some. A few may want to spend a year at some private high school that has a "post-graduate year" program for those who want to strengthen their academic preparation before tackling college. Both kinds of institutions can tell you about the various financial aid programs available to cover your tuition and living expenses. This aid may come from the school itself or from a variety of government and foundation programs.

Some liberal arts colleges and universities offer a crash

course on basic skills during the summer between high school and college, either for everyone or especially for minority students. These courses may be useful if you are already close to meeting the normal standards of the school and just need a little extra to put you over the top. But a summer is far too short to remedy years of sub-standard ghetto education. Relying on a summer crash course can be a prelude to crashing during the academic year.

A whole year spent working full-time on what you missed in high school is not too much. It may be the best investment of your life. It will mean graduating from college a year later—but that is far better than not graduating at all, or graduating only by taking the easier courses and missing many opportunities you might have been able to master if you had had a solid educational background behind you. As it is now, many minority students end up taking five or more years to complete a four-year college, because they discover the hard way that they cannot take a full load of courses and still keep up with the assignments. It is far better to take an extra year beforehand, to be able to handle the normal requirements in the normal way.

Younger Children

Minority parents sometimes get a second chance after they recover from the shock of discovering the gross inadequacy of the education received by their young man or young woman who is about to enter college. It can alert these parents to do something about the education of their younger children before they reach this point. "We can't wait until students are juniors and seniors in high school before talking to them about college," as the Dean of Admissions at Syracuse University said. "By that time, about the only thing you have to discuss is all the things they should have done when they were younger." Minority parents, especially, have to find out what can be done at an earlier stage, because often the public schools in minority neighborhoods fail as badly in counseling as they do in education.

Among the alternatives to a substandard public school are (1) transfer to a better public school elsewhere, if possible; (2) transfer to a private day school, in the neighborhood or away; or (3) transfer to a private boarding school, which may be located hundreds of miles away. Given the limited income of most minority families, options (2) and (3) may seem impossible. But they may not be.

It is obviously hard to try to send children off to private boarding schools because financial aid is much more scarce in private elementary or high schools than in college. However, some will be able to do this. An organization for minority students called A Better Chance, located in Boston but operating nationwide, can be helpful for those who want to try this route. Other parents will find a variety of other options.

Many minority parents may never think of private schools for their children because "private schools" conjures up the image of posh boarding schools for the rich, located on hundreds of acres of land, and costing upwards of $10,000 a year. This is a true picture as regards places like Exeter and Andover, but most private schools are nothing like Exeter and Andover. According to official U.S. Department of Education statistics, nearly one-fifth of all private elementary schools in the United States charged less than $500 a year in 1985–1986. That's less than $50 a month, and it can usually be paid in installments, just as people buy furniture and appliances on the installment plan.

At the high school level, tuition goes up significantly, on

average. However, for high school as for college, you need only one. Moreover, at least partial financial aid is available, and an older child can contribute to his own tuition from his summer earnings. The summer earnings of a teenager making the minimum wage would cover the full tuition for a year at many private high schools, even if the parents contributed nothing and the school refused to give any financial aid. With just a small amount of help from a working-class family, it is very do-able. At the very least, do not dismiss the possibility without looking into the specifics. Getting a decent education in ghetto high schools is far harder, and trying to make it through a good college without a decent educational background is courting disaster, personal as well as educational.

Social adjustments that might be a strain at posh places like Exeter and Andover may not be nearly as difficult at low-cost private schools, where fellow students are also likely to be from modest income levels. There are private, all-black schools in Harlem, as well as in other ghettos from coast to coast. Even where the schools are racially integrated, the white students are more likely to be the children of carpenters or clerks, rather than the children of doctors or stockbrokers. Since most of these schools are day schools, rather than boarding schools, there is no adjustment to living with people from different backgrounds 24 hours a day, as there is at college. It could be a good transition, especially for black students with very little experience in dealing with people from other racial backgrounds.

Will private schools make a difference? Obviously, it depends on the individual. But a study by Professor James Coleman of the University of Chicago indicates that private schools improve the academic performance of black students even more than they improve the academic performance of white students.

Campus Visits

Campus visits are even more important for minority parents and students than they are for others. There is no better way to tell how the local white students will react to a black student than by confronting them with a black student and seeing what they say or do. This is especially important in those parts of the United States where many of the white students have never interacted with blacks, and in fact know blacks chiefly from watching television. Even in parts of the country where there is racial diversity in the population, a particular college may draw the bulk of its students from affluent white suburbs. This does not mean that they will be racists, but there may be differences in social background that may be hard to bridge—or maybe not. Being there is the best way to judge.

One of the things to look for during your visit is whether the black students are mingled in with other students on campus or can be seen walking around in separate groups, eating lunch at separate tables, and perhaps rooming together in the dorm or even being housed together in a separate dorm. Whether you regard such patterns as solidarity or separatism, you need to know whether or not they exist—and how that fits in with your own idea of what a college experience should be.

Many colleges and universities have a Black Students Union or similar organization. It can be very useful to talk to members and leaders of this organization during a campus visit, whether or not you would expect to join after entering college. The kind of leaders and the nature of the organization can have a deep influence on the whole racial atmosphere on campus, which in turn affects even those black students who do not belong. If their policies and actions create racial polarization, for example, you are going to feel it, whether you had anything to do with it or not. If the BSU plays a more positive role in helping black students adjust to the campus and the classroom, you will be a beneficiary of a better atmosphere, whether or not you yourself need such help in adjusting. Meeting the people involved can give you better information than you can get from any other source and you will know better than anyone else how well their ideas fit in with yours.

Parents

Parents can be very important during the campus visit, if they can afford to come along. While the student is on campus, the parents can circulate through the local community, getting impressions of the people and of their reactions to blacks. This may be especially important on a distant campus, in an unfamiliar part of the country, and where there are relatively few blacks living in the local community. It can be a very worthwhile investment to set aside 10 or 20 dollars to make a large number of small purchases in various stores, shops, and restaurants, just to interact and get into conversation with local people.

If there is a local black community, some of these interactions should take place there. People in barbershops and beauty parlors seldom need much encouragement to talk, and a shoe shine or a shampoo may be enough reason to go in. Just mentioning that you are in town looking over the local college may be enough to bring out information about the atmosphere on campus and in town. If you go into a local fast-food place or other business during the slow hours, you have a good chance of finding people ready to talk. Informal and unofficial sources of information can be especially important to minority students and parents because there are so many taboos and shibboleths about race among college officials.

Not everyone can afford a campus visit, and even among those who can, there may be strict limits on how many campuses can be visited, how far away, and whether parents can afford to go along on all the visits. If a parent can afford to accompany the student to a college relatively close by but not one a thousand miles away, it may be a good strategy to visit the closer campus first. After students and parents take notes on what they see, at the college and in the local community, they may want to talk over what they found out very carefully, so that the student alone can cover many of the same things on the distant campus.

Where finances make even one campus visit doubtful, the cost should be checked out before writing off the possibility. Many colleges allow a free overnight stay in the dorms for the student and this is a very desirable experience anyway, as a means of collecting information and impressions. Inexpensive lodgings may be available for parents on campus or off. Motels in small college towns are often much less expensive than in big cities. If you can afford it, you will probably get your money's worth from a campus visit. Avoiding a situation that would be intolerable is worth a lot. So too is discovering a place where your academic development can flourish in an environment that also offers a fulfilling social development.

Athletics

Virtually all colleges have athletic programs of one sort or another. But, like everything else, they vary enormously. On some campuses, especially among small liberal arts colleges, a large part of the student body participates in intramural sports for recreation and exercise. For those who enjoy sports, there is no real problem with this kind of casual athletic competition. There can be very serious problems, however, with big-time athletics of the sort that brings huge crowds to the stadium and may be televised to millions of viewers across the country. To some minority students, athletics presents a tempting way to go to college. But there is a lot to think about—very seriously— underneath the glitter and glamour.

Anyone who follows sports knows that blacks are heavily represented among both collegiate and professional athletes, and especially among the star athletes. The enormous salaries and tremendous publicity surrounding a relative handful of sports celebrities makes athletics seem far more promising than it is. The grim truth is that more than 90 percent of all college athletes in football, baseball, and basketball never sign a professional contract, much less have a career in sports.

In absolute numbers, less than 3,000 black people in the whole country make a living in these three sports combined—and that is counting players in major leagues, minor leagues, and semi-pro play, as well as coaches, trainers, and the like. This is not a realistic prospect for millions of black youngsters.

If all that was likely to happen if you became a college athlete was that your sports career wouldn't go any further, that would be just one of life's many disappointments. Often, it is far worse than that. The demanding life of an athlete—the practice, the travel, the time spent studying plays—can leave very little time and energy for learning anything academic. Four years of your life spent entertaining other people in a stadium can easily end up with you

out on the street with absolutely nothing to show for it—
no degree, no sports contract, no money, and no job skill
on which to build a career. However much publicity and
popularity you may have had on campus while playing,
you can find yourself quickly forgotten by your former
classmates as they go on up the ladder in their careers.

College athletics is a prime example of a situation where
other people's agendas can destroy your agenda. The
coach's agenda is to win—at all costs. Coaches are paid very
well for winning and are fired very quickly for losing.
Under these conditions, it is completely unrealistic to
expect most coaches to be concerned about your education.
On the contrary, the coach's main concern may be to stop
you from taking "too many" solid academic courses that
will take up time that he wants you to spend in practice,
in body conditioning, and in learning the team's
plays.

Although professional football players almost all came
out of colleges, and are identified with those colleges, the
great majority of National Football League players never
graduated from college. The same is true in other sports.
Of 18 first-round collegiate draft choices in the National
Basketball Association in 1986, less than half had actually
graduated. Among the minority who did receive a degree,
not one majored in math, English, engineering, philosophy,
or any of the sciences. Most majored in easy Mickey Mouse
subjects.

Coach Joe Paterno of Penn State perhaps summed up
the situation best when he said: "It has always been my
opinion that *the* most important thing an athlete receives
here at Penn State is his or her degree. The degree tran-
scends everything else, including undefeated seasons or
Bowl trips, All-American recognition, even winning a Na-

tional championship. None of those things take the place of a good education."

Do not expect to find a lot of Joe Paternos in this world. Certainly don't bet your education and your future on finding another one.

Black Colleges

Although most black students no longer go to black colleges, a sizeable number still do. There are more than 80 institutions in which over half the student body is black. Some are institutions established historically for the specific purpose of serving black students: Howard University, Tuskegee Institute, Fisk University, and the Atlanta University complex, including Morehouse, Spelman, and Morris Brown colleges, for example. Others include colleges and universities established more recently that became predominantly black because of where they were located—the University of the District of Columbia, for example—or simply because black students were disproportionately attracted to their programs.

In theory, there are black colleges and white colleges, but in reality things have become more complicated. There are white students on many traditionally black campuses today, and thousands of black students on some white campuses. West Virginia State College was initially founded in 1891 to serve black students, but today most of its students are white. Conversely, the Brooklyn campus of Long Island University is less than half white today, though other campuses of L.I.U. remain predominantly white. In absolute numbers, there are more black students at Wayne State University than there are at Fisk, Hampton, Tuskegee, or most other black colleges and universities.

All this relates to your reason for wanting to go to a

black college. If your purpose is to socialize with large numbers of other black students, then that can be done as easily at Wayne State or the Brooklyn campus of L.I.U. as it can at the traditionally black colleges. However, if what you really want is a whole environment that is overwhelmingly and traditionally black, then your attention must turn to institutions like Howard, Fisk, Morehouse, Spelman, and Tuskegee.

Many black students will find that the academic standards and test score levels at black colleges match their own academic levels better than some other colleges do. Whether there is a match in other ways, such as in values and lifestyle, will depend upon the specifics of particular black colleges. You cannot assume that there will automatically be a match, just because the other students are black.

On the other hand, for black students with strong academic backgrounds and composite S.A.T.'s above 1000, *there are simply no black colleges to match them with academically*. Many such students—especially those who have grown tired of always being in a small minority in predominantly white schools—often want to believe that there are black colleges to match the Ivy League or other top-tier institutions. But the facts contradict this belief or wish. Every black institution in the United States has an S.A.T. level below the national average. Howard University has long been regarded as first among the black colleges and universities, but less than half the Howard faculty have Ph.D.'s and less than half the Howard students have graduated five years after they enter.

The historic role of the black colleges in creating a black educated class, the struggles these institutions had to undergo merely to survive, the many distinguished black scholars they had at one time, when they were the only places where such scholars could teach, have all combined to create a feeling of pride, loyalty, and mystique. But when you are choosing a college, the only colleges you can attend are the ones that actually exist today, as they really are today—not the legends that have come down through the years or the visions you may have in your mind.

Cutting through the images to the reality is especially important, and especially difficult, in the case of the black colleges. Neither high school counselors nor the authors of college guides want to be accused of racism for saying critical things about them. Most college guides, even those that can be critical or even sarcastic about other institutions, tend to be either bland or gushing about black colleges. Edward B. Fiske's *Selective Guide to the Colleges* is exceptional and tries in a gentle way to convey some of the realities about the black institutions. A campus visit, with well-planned note-taking, is even more important in the case of black colleges than for colleges in general.

✔ ASIAN AMERICANS

The situation of Asian Americans is very different from that of blacks, Hispanics, or American Indians. Whereas these latter disadvantaged groups tend to score below the general population on tests and to have poorer academic records in general, Asian Americans tend to at least hold their own in general and to excel in mathematics and science.

Despite many spectacular success stories among Asian Americans—both native-born and immigrants—the *average* Asian American student is not spectacular. In 1987, Asian Americans averaged 405 on the verbal S.A.T. and

521 on the math S.A.T., compared to the national average of 430 verbal and 476 in math. Asian American students' below-average verbal and above-average math scores add up to a composite S.A.T. total just 20 points above the national average. However, it takes only a modest difference in averages between two groups to translate into substantial differences in representation at the extremes. Less than 4 percent of all students have a quantitative S.A.T. score of 700 or above, but more than 9 percent of all Asian students reach this level.

Asian Americans are accordingly very much over-represented in institutions with very high math S.A.T.'s. Asian Americans are about one-fifth of all students at Cal Tech and at M.I.T., and two-fifths of all engineering students at Berkeley. Although only about 2 percent of the population, Asian Americans receive 17 percent of all engineering Ph.D.'s in the United States. Of 70 scholarship winners in the prestigious Westinghouse Talent Search from 1981 to 1987, 20 were Asian Americans.

The academic success of Asian Americans is reminiscent of the rapid academic rise of Jewish immigrant children earlier in this century. Also reminiscent of that era are the limits that seem to be set against their increased admission to some leading colleges and universities. No one has admitted to setting quota limits for Asians but suspicious things have happened in many institutions in recent years.

The percentage of Asian applicants to Berkeley who were admitted was cut in half—from 62 percent to 31 percent—in just 5 years. At Brown University, the admission rate for Asian American applicants in 1983 was less than one-third of what it was in 1975. The number of Asian Americans in Princeton's freshman class in 1986 was 25 percent lower than it was just the year before. At Harvard, white and Asian applicants had very similar test scores but, among those admitted, Asians had test scores more than a hundred points higher than whites, suggesting that they had to be better to get in.

At Amherst, 40 percent of black applicants and 43 percent of Hispanic applicants were accepted for the class of 1991, but only 25 percent of Asian American applicants were accepted. If other minority groups had higher academic performances than Asian Americans, that would be understandable. But all the evidence says just the opposite.

Given that man's sins are unlimited, while your time is not, how much time and effort does it pay an Asian American high school student to invest in worrying about this? Probably not much. The representation of Asian American students remains high at leading colleges, universities, and engineering schools across the country. There are more than a hundred institutions where more than 10 percent of the students are Asian Americans. Moreover, the proportions of Asian American students are rising sharply at some institutions while they are falling at others. The numbers of Asian American students have more than doubled over a period of five years at Cornell and Ohio State, and more than doubled in one year at Stanford. In over-all effect, quota ceilings are as petty as they are dishonorable. Quotas did not stop the rise of the Jews and they are not going to stop the rise of Asian Americans.

On a personal, practical level, if you were planning to apply to five institutions, it may be worthwhile to apply to six, to make allowance for any quota ceiling somewhere. Beyond that, it is not worth worrying about. Above all, make a clear distinction between the administrators who handle admissions decisions and the faculty who will be teaching you. Whatever political considerations or sociological fads lead to quota ceilings among administrators, professors are almost always glad to see good students, and Asian American students have long established an academic record that makes them welcome in the classroom. Once you are in college, your education largely depends on you and the faculty. You may never see anyone from the admissions office the whole time you are there.

PART II:

WHAT TO DO

CHAPTER 8

GETTING STARTED

Organizing what you are going to do is the key to keeping your sanity while trying to cope simultaneously with the problems of choosing a college, finishing high school, and taking care of many other details and problems that come crowding in on you all at once. There is no point trying to think through all the issues and possibilities together. Simplifying what you have to do into steps can help you turn your attention to one complication at a time. The easiest way to do this may be to make a list, showing what you need to do, and in what sequence. Among the things on that list should be:

1. Taking a college entrance examination, whether the Scholastic Aptitude Test (S.A.T.) or an examination from the American College Testing program (A.C.T.).
2. Buying several college guides of different types.
3. Determining what general kinds of institutions best suit you: colleges, universities, or institutes of technology, for example.
4. Consulting with high school teachers and counselors—*after*

you have already gotten some preliminary ideas and information on your own.

5. Determining what special personal requirements you may have as to geographic region, campus atmosphere, financial arrangements, and the like.

6. Sending for college catalogues (from perhaps 10–20 places) after you have begun to narrow your choices.

7. Attending high school meetings at which representatives from various colleges speak.

8. Making campus visits to some of the institutions you are seriously considering, if that is practical.

9. Applying to several colleges and then making your choice among those that accept you.

Let us consider these steps in turn, in this chapter and in the chapters that follow.

✔ TEST SCORES

There is so much to do during the senior year of high school—and so many deadlines to meet—that the long process of choosing a college should begin during the junior year, if possible. Some college application deadlines are as early as November 30th (for the University of California system), which gives you very little time for all the things that must be done between the opening of high school in September and the time when test results, transcripts, letters of recommendation, and other material must be on file with colleges. Most selective institutions have application deadlines somewhere between January 1st (at Harvard and M.I.T.) and March 1st (at Whitman or at Dickinson). This might seem to be a comfortable amount of time, but often it isn't.

A couple of months can elapse between the time a student applies to take the Scholastic Aptitude Test and the time when the results are tabulated and sent out. For example, to take the first S.A.T. examination of the academic year, usually held in early October, the student must apply to the College Board in early September—which is to say, shortly after school opens. Until the results come back in early November, you are missing a key piece of information needed to decide which kinds of colleges it would make sense to apply to. If the whole process of investigating colleges and deciding where to apply begins at that point, it can be quite a scramble to make a decision and get all the transcripts, recommendations, and other material sent off to these institutions before the Christmas vacation begins, so that this will all be in their hands in time for January deadlines. Seldom does every detail go exactly according to plan. If you have to go back and remind someone to send a letter of recommendation, or keep after the high school officials to put your transcript in the mail to the colleges, it may be tough to make even a February deadline.

It will take a lot of needless pressure off if you first take the S.A.T. (or the A.C.T.) during your junior year, to get some idea where you stand scholastically. The results will enable you to compare yourself to national norms, as the colleges do, instead of trying to guess how the grades at your high school compare to grades at other schools elsewhere. An early test also allows for unforeseeable events. You may have the flu or some other problem on the day the S.A.T. or A.C.T. is given and not do your best. Taking the test in your junior year allows you to schedule another test later on, when you are feeling better. But if you wait until your senior year, and then take the last test that will make the college application deadline, whatever goes wrong on that test will be set in concrete.

Even if all goes well on the S.A.T. or A.C.T. test during your junior year, it is still a good idea to take it again in your senior year. You will have learned more by then and will be more familiar with the exam as well. What the first set of scores does is to give you a fix on where you stand. It also gives you several months in which to start thinking things over and talking them over with parents, teachers, and others, before the senior year begins.

Many things besides test scores must be taken into account before a final decision is made, either by you or by the colleges to which you apply. But the foundation, the bedrock, on which all this sits is your academic performance and capability. Since nobody can get inside your head, the next best thing is to look at high school grades and test scores. That must be your starting point as well.

In recent years, it has become fashionable to say that test scores don't "really" matter that much. In exactly the same sense, some people say that height isn't "really" that important in basketball and "speed isn't everything" in a wide receiver in football. For that matter, "money isn't everything"—but no one who is destitute is likely to kid himself that it isn't important. Test scores matter, even to many who say they don't matter. They can matter catastrophically to those students who ignore them in choosing a college.

This is not to say that test scores are the be-all and end-all. In fact, they are just the beginning of the process of weeding out possibilities. But they are a necessary beginning.

Once you have determined which colleges, universities, or technical institutes are within your scholastic range, you can then begin to weigh the other considerations which will determine how many of these institutions are worth further investigation. At this point—hopefully, before the senior year of high school begins—you can sit down with a piece of paper, perhaps parents and student together, to write down some of the many factors to consider and discuss. At this point, some college guides may be very helpful.

✔ COLLEGE GUIDES AND RANKINGS

Kinds of Guides

Perhaps the best kinds of general college guides to begin with are those with brief descriptions and opinions about 200 or 300 colleges, universities, and technical institutes. These are usually easy reading, sometimes entertaining, and often have a telling sentence or two that will either excite your interest in a particular college or let you know that this is a place you want to avoid like the plague. Usually these kinds of guides also include a very few key statistics, such as the average S.A.T. or A.C.T. score at each institution, the total number of students, and the tuition.

For those primarily interested in the more selective institutions, the best of these kinds of college guides are *The Insider's Guide to the Colleges*, published annually by the *Yale Daily News*, and *Selective Guide to Colleges*, written by Edward B. Fiske, education editor of the *New York Times*. Another guide written by Fiske is called *The Best Buys in College Education*. As the title suggests, it concentrates on institutions whose tuition costs are not as horrendous as others. Although the colleges listed in the latter overlap with those covered in Fiske's other book, the guide to lower-cost institutions not only includes top-rated places like the University of Chicago and the University of California at Berkeley, but also more modestly ranked institutions like Rockford College and Hillsdale College. In fact, given the large-scale financial aid available at most expensive institutions, for many students the principal value of *The Best Buys in College Education* is that it gives descriptions and insights into a wider academic range of colleges.

Another kind of college guide is that chock-full of statistics and other information of a sort that means nothing by itself, but which can be very valuable after you have some framework to put it in. These guides may cover 10 times as many institutions as the descriptive guides mentioned above. The *College Handbook*, published by the College Board, lists information on more than 3,000 four-year colleges. Guides of this sort are strictly reference books— no one in his right mind would try to read through them— and become useful only after you have already developed an interest in particular institutions and want to dig further into the facts about them. Since even these huge guides are usually available in paperback editions for less than $20, it is probably a very good investment to get at least one. When you consider the high cost of a college education, buying half a dozen guides to help you make your choice would not be an extravagance.

My favorite among the big blockbuster type of guides is *The Comparative Guide to American Colleges* by James Cass and Max Birnbaum. However, a lot could be said for *Barron's Profiles of American Colleges* or *Lovejoy's College Guide*. What strikes me about the Cass and Birnbaum guide is that it doesn't go to the extreme of the "just-the-facts" approach. For example, in the midst of its statistics, it characterizes the student body at Whitman College as "overwhelmingly scholarly and intellectual" and Lafayette

College students as "primarily oriented toward occupational/professional goals." Many colleges, however, it doesn't characterize at all. The amount of attention and space it gives varies with the academic standing or visibility of the institution—not how many people are likely to go there. The University of Chicago, for example, gets almost twice as much space as Southern Illinois University, which has three times as many students.

The huge guides in general tell you things that the smaller descriptive guides simply do not have space for. The Cass and Birnbaum guide, for example, tells you what percentage of the entering freshmen at various colleges come from what regions of the country, how many freshmen return for their sophomore year, what percentage graduate, and what percentage of graduates go on to medical school, law school, etc. Even though these and other facts may not all be significant in every case, it is significant when a guide reports that 37 percent of the freshmen at Bennington College do not return for the sophomore year and only 41 percent graduate. Conversely, it is also significant that only 8 percent of Muhlenberg College's freshmen fail to return for their sophomore years, and that 82 percent of the students graduate. Some will find it significant that two-thirds of the students at Skidmore College are women while a similar percentage at Union College are men. To those thinking in terms of marital prospects, these are more than dry statistics.

In general, the numbers in large, heavily statistical guides will mean something only after you have clarified in your own mind just what it is you are looking for. Reading the smaller descriptive guides can help bring you to that point, as will discussions with parents, teachers, and others. For those who are confining their search to some of the higher-rated or better-known colleges, a smaller statistical guide that can be very useful is *Peterson's Competitive Colleges*.

Among the more specialized guides, *The Black Student's Guide to Colleges* has an obvious constituency, despite its shortcomings. *Lisa Birnbach's College Book* has a very different constituency—the affluent and "with it" crowd. Her comments on drugs and homosexuality at various colleges, however, may be of interest to many parents and students who are not with it, as well as to those who are. Conservative parents may be reassured by Lisa Birnbach's comments on "the gay situation" at some colleges ("No gays that anyone knows of" at Wabash College or at Sweet Briar) or the favorite drugs ("Vitamin C" at Oral Roberts University). They are less likely to be reassured after reading what is said about drugs at Reed and Bard or about homosexuality at Smith, Mills, Yale, and Chicago. Still, they may be glad that they found out sooner rather than later—and on paper rather than in real life.

While some college guides are better than others for some purposes, the only one that should be condemned outright is *America's Best Colleges*, which is easily America's worst college guide. What makes this guide special are its lists of the "best" institutions in various categories, reprinted from *U.S. News & World Report* magazine, which is also the publisher of the guide. Widespread criticism of the shabby way these lists were compiled have come even from presidents of universities rated in the top 10 by this publication. Usually, only the losers criticize rankings, but when the winners also criticize, you know that something is seriously wrong. At Stanford University—ranked number one by *U.S. News & World Report*—both the president and the director of admissions publicly questioned the way the rankings were done.

Instead of getting your own college guides, catalogues, and brochures, you may be able to read those in public libraries or in the offices of high school counselors. However, these may or may not be up-to-date. Those in some public libraries may be several years out of date. Most colleges and universities don't change that much in a few years—except for tuition, which is no small exception. It may be useful to check out the dates of the catalogues and brochures in your high school counselor's office, as a way of checking out the high school counselor. Any counselor who hasn't made the small effort required to get up-to-date material from the colleges may be bad news in other ways, and it is better to discover that early on.

It may seem cheaper to read college guides in a public library, rather than buy them, but it is a false economy. If you start out with a long list of "possible" colleges and proceed to reduce it to a small list of "likely" ones, then there may be a significant amount of reading to do and it should not be crammed. Too much is at stake. Guides that are in your home can be read whenever the time and the mood are right, over a period of weeks and months. Special things about particular colleges can be underlined and comments put in the margins, to be looked at perhaps months later, when you are ready to decide where to send applications—and still later again, when making your final choice among the colleges that accepted you.

Reading college guides in libraries, or on loan for a few weeks, means giving up these advantages and relying on memory. Unless your memory is phenomenal, it is penny-wise and pound-foolish to save a few dollars like this on as big an investment as a college. Even if someone else pays for college, it is still a very big investment of your time, emotions, and future.

Rankings

Because there are many useless and misleading rankings in print, it is worth exploring what is wrong with the lists in *America's Best Colleges*, so as to have some idea how to evaluate the validity of other rankings. The lists were based on selections by college and university presidents who were each asked by *U.S. News & World Report* to name his or her own "top 10" in one category or another. The criteria suggested were "cohesiveness of the curriculum, quality of teaching, relationship between faculty and students and the overall atmosphere of learning fostered by the campus."

These are good criteria, but it is completely unrealistic to expect busy college presidents to be able to apply them to other colleges. Presidents of huge universities with 30,000 or 40,000 students might have trouble applying these criteria on their own campuses. How many presidents of colleges or universities on the east coast have ever set foot in a classroom at Berkeley or U.C.L.A.? For that matter, how many presidents of Harvard have ever sat in on classes at M.I.T., two subway stops away?

To their credit, 40 percent of the college presidents did not reply to the questionnaire sent them by *U.S. News & World Report*, and some took the trouble to write the magazine to object to the whole procedure. The president of Middlebury College, for example, wrote: "I seriously doubt that any of us had anything more than a superficial knowledge of most other campuses." Other college presidents also refused to send in their rankings on similar grounds. Those college presidents who did send in their rankings may well have found it easier to list 10 institutions off the top of their heads than to explain why they would not do so.

Unfortunately, many parents and students may have taken such rankings seriously. What each person really needs is his or her own "top 10" or top 5, as the case may be. The list of the best colleges or universities for one individual will seldom be the same for another, even if they are brothers or sisters.

Some rankings, however, are based on much better knowledge. Rankings of specific departments usually have a much more solid basis than the rankings of whole colleges or universities. When chemists rank chemistry departments and economists rank economics departments, they are in a position to know what they are talking about. They may know the professors (either personally or through their writings or participation in professional conferences) and they may know how well prepared the students are when they go on to post-graduate education. Even without setting foot in a particular college's classrooms, a graduate school professor who always finds the students from a particular college thoroughly familiar with their subject knows that there is good teaching going on there.

When little-known Davidson College is ranked among the top dozen in the country by law school deans for the quality of its students who go on to law school, the deans probably know what they are talking about—and this is valuable information about the college, even if you have no intention of going to law school. Similarly, it is probably a well-informed judgment when the deans of graduate schools of engineering include Rose-Hulman Institute and Harvey Mudd College among the top 15 institutions in the quality of their engineering graduates. Their assessment may be particularly valuable if you have never heard of either of these schools before.

Most rankings of departments are rankings of *graduate* departments of universities, and these may be of limited value to undergraduates. However, there are also rankings of colleges according to the number or percentage of their graduates who continue on to receive a Ph.D. Some of these have already been indicated in earlier chapters, though for a limited number of institutions. A much fuller list is available in the November/December 1986 issue of *Change* magazine.

An even longer list of several hundred private, four-year colleges, ranked by the absolute number of doctorates received by their graduates, is available in a publication called *Baccalaureate Origins of Doctorate Recipients: A Ranking by Discipline of 4-Year Private Institutions*. It is issued by the Office of Institutional Research at Franklin & Marshall College. Like other statistics, these are useful to the extent that you remember their limitations—in this case, that there are no adjustments for institutional size and that universities and state colleges are omitted. Even with these limitations in mind, however, you may find the large number of colleges covered to be useful to you, especially if you are considering a college not likely to be on shorter lists. It can be very enlightening, for example, to discover that Middlebury College graduates received far more doctorates in a decade than the graduates of Bennington College received in more than 60 years.

If you would like the same data for all colleges, universities, engineering schools, and military academies—total and broken down by sex of students—and are prepared to pay $100 for it, you can get elaborate print-outs of this data from the National Research Council in Washington,

D.C. Probably only some professional guidance counselors or university research scholars would want to go this far. But, if you have the curiosity and the money, just ask for the bound volume of print-outs called *Baccalaureate Origins of Doctorate Recipients from U.S. Universities.* The title is similar to that of the smaller compilation by Franklin & Marshall College because they are drawn from the same source. Incidentally, it should not be surprising to discover that Franklin & Marshall usually makes a very good showing in these lists.

"Selectivity"

One of the most elusive concepts appearing in various college guides is "selectivity." Supposedly, it refers to how difficult it is to get admitted to a particular college. Phrases like "competitive," "highly competitive," or "non-competitive" are used to rank colleges by their selectivity. Unfortunately, different guides rank the same colleges differently. Chapman College is ranked above the University of California at Davis by *The ARCO Guide: The Right College*, Chapman being "competitive" and U.C. Davis being "non-competitive," according to them. But Cass and Birnbaum give just the reverse ranking in their *Comparative Guide to American Colleges*. Chapman receives no selectivity rating, while U.C. Davis is rated "Selective +." *Barron's Profiles of American Colleges* rates Chapman "Competitive" and U.C. Davis "Competitive +."

There are by no means the only inconsistent rankings of the "selectivity" of the same institutions by different college guides. Georgia Tech ranks above Harvey Mudd in *The Right College*, but they are ranked just the opposite in Cass and Birnbaum. Whitman versus Antioch, or Brigham Young versus Arizona State, would also turn out to produce opposite selectivity rankings in these two guides. As you expand the number of institutions and the number of guides, the inconsistencies multiply.

The underlying problem is that "selectivity" often has no concrete criteria and changes meaning as readily as a chameleon changes color. If half the people who apply to a given college are admitted, that tells you very little by itself, without further investigation. College A and college B may both admit half their applicants, but if college A is a high quality institution, whose courses are very demanding, then highly qualified students are likely to apply. If college B is an easygoing party school, it may attract so many applicants with very poor qualifications that it has to turn away half of them. If "selectivity" is judged on some purely statistical basis, A and B are the same—even though any given person would find it harder to get into A than into B.

Location can also affect how many people apply, and therefore what percentage was accepted. A college located in the heart of New York City or Chicago is almost certain to be noticed and applied to, just because it is so near to so many people. But almost no one applies to Whitman College because it happens to be nearby—because it is not nearby to anything, except the small town of Walla Walla, Washington. People apply to Whitman because they have heard good things about that particular college. Because it accepts most of its applicants does not mean that it is easy to get into, since it tends to attract serious students with good academic records. Clemson University accepts a smaller percentage of its applicants than Whitman does, but the Whitman applicants have higher test scores. What really matters about any college is how easy it is for *you* to get in, not what percentage of other people got in.

Opaque rankings of "selectivity" or "competitiveness" in admissions can be misleading as far as the practical question of your own admissions chances is concerned. Trying to determine whether your S.A.T. scores and high school grades are about what the other students admitted had is likely to give you a better idea of your chances. *Barron's Profiles of American Colleges* explains the basis of its admissions rankings in these terms so as to facilitate such comparisons. However, even the best estimate remains only an estimate, because of the large element of chance in the admissions process.

What a good estimate can do is show a range of colleges where your chances of acceptance are good and where most of the other students come from the same general range of academic capabilities. This is important not only for getting admitted but also for doing your best afterwards. Professors tend to teach to the level of their students, whether intentionally or by a process of adjustment of their expectations. There is no point finding yourself in a situation where you are always trailing the pack—or in the opposite situation, where you must endure an agonizingly slow pace and repeated explanations of things you understood long ago. The practical purpose of trying to understand a college's admissions standards is to try to make the right match, not to rank institutions in prestige or in some other abstract sense.

CHAPTER 9

WEEDING OUT

Every step leading up to college applications is essentially a weeding out process. When you take the S.A.T. or A.C.T. and get your own test scores back, these alone may eliminate hundreds—or even thousands—of colleges above or below your academic range. To continue this process you need to develop your own list of requirements, preferences, aversions, as well as a sense of your own strengths, blind spots, and areas you want to work on. Most people will get more insight through talking all this over with other people, even if those other people have no concrete information or suggestions to offer on specific colleges. As you have repeated talks with parents, teachers, friends of the family, high school counselors, and others, it may become clearer that certain kinds of colleges would be very desirable for you and certain other kinds very undesirable, whether for academic, social, or personal reasons.

Perhaps you don't want to be too far from home—or perhaps you need to put a lot of distance between you and home, to develop independence and find your own way.

Maybe the money situation will determine what is practical and what is not. The kinds of people who go to some colleges may make these particular institutions especially attractive—or out of the question. Sometimes you will know people who have gone to specific colleges and who can give you first-hand information and impressions.

This exploratory phase should start no later than your junior year of high school, when there is plenty of time to talk things over with many people, without having to reach any conclusion or commit yourself. If you change your mind several times along the way, and re-arrange your priorities, that probably means you are discovering things you wouldn't have thought of at first, so the whole process is proving to be worthwhile. Nothing is worse than getting a fixed idea and sticking to it stubbornly, in spite of anything, just for the feeling of being decisive. That way you can paint yourself into a corner. Listening does not mean obeying. It means finding out. You can learn some important things even from someone whose conclusions you reject.

Only after you have gotten some general ideas from your test scores, from conversations with family and friends, and from reading a little in college guides, should you seek the advice of a "professional," such as a teacher or counselor. You will be able to ask better questions, carry on a dialogue—and not become someone being blindly led. You may also be better able to form some idea of the counselor's own knowledge and depth of understanding. If you have been fortunate enough to find someone who understands colleges and understands you, you may be able to strike a number of schools off your list immediately, add some you hadn't thought of, and know what to look for when thinking about some others.

It is important to avoid letting anyone become your one and only guru from the outset—especially if that seems to be a role he or she relishes. You need a "second opinion"—and a third opinion, and fourth opinion, if you can get them. There may be quite a few worthwhile opinions available, if you stop and think about possible sources. Relatives, family friends, teachers, and others who have gone to college may be worth having some conversations with, even if they have no specific suggestions. Sometimes even people who have never been to any college may have some useful input if they know you well. If your mother never went to college, she probably can't tell you whether Johns Hopkins is better than Cornell, but if you talk over the various differences between them with her, she may be able to tell you things about yourself that may make it easier for you to determine whether John Hopkins or Cornell is better for you.

As things begin to sort themselves out in your mind—as you begin to decide what kinds of institutions you would like, what kind of environment you want, what you can realistically afford—then it will be time to look more closely at particular places to determine how well they approximate what you are looking for. At that point, you need to look more closely at various kinds of literature and, if possible, at the campuses themselves.

✔ BROCHURES

Nothing is easier than getting brochures from colleges and you may be inundated with them if you get on some mailing list. These brochures are often gems of the advertising art and as seductive as your favorite heart-throb. Photographs of beautiful campus scenes are usually interspersed with photos of students and their professors in warm, soulful communion, often accompanied by pithy quotes about how wonderful it is to be at Ivy University or Podunk A&M. On the surface, they all seem alike, and yet a careful reading of brochures—and still more so, of catalogues—can reveal important differences.

College brochures, in addition to pretty pictures and glowing generalities about commitment to education and high ideals, also contain some useful factual information. Some tell you what percentage of applicants are admitted from various S.A.T. score levels. Some tell you what percentage of students from various income levels receive financial aid. Some tell you what percentage of their graduates who apply to medical school or law school are admitted. They are especially likely to give you such statistics if they are favorable. When 90 percent of Carleton College's graduates who apply to medical school are accepted (and an even higher percentage to law school), they are not likely to keep that secret. When a college has been praised in various guides and surveys, that fact also tends to find its way into their brochures. But when a college brochure consists of nothing but fine photographs and glowing words, that should raise a question as to why there isn't any hard news.

A red marking pen is useful for outlining a few key facts scattered here and there among the lofty and smarmy rhetoric. When you find a brochure with nothing to outline, that tells you something.

The brochure for Franklin & Marshall College gives the high national rankings of various departments of theirs. Even without explicit rankings of colleges or departments, however, it is often possible to get some idea of their quality from their students' acceptance rates into medical

schools and law schools, or into "3–2" engineering programs. Even without knowing anything about the quality
of the math department at Whitman College or at Occidental College, you may draw some inferences from the fact
that both these institutions have "3–2" programs with Cal
Tech.

Colleges with special programs often explain those programs in their brochures. Kalamazoo College, for example,
has a special "career development internship" program
which is an integral part of its education. In the last quarter
of the sophomore year a student goes off to work on a job
related to his or her field of study, and then returns to
college for the summer quarter to make up the academic
work. This may not be everyone's cup of tea, but for some
students it can be very valuable, not only as a source of
money, but also as a preview of a particular career and an
opportunity to mature on their own, away from both home
and college, for a brief time in a selected situation. The
brochure is valuable, whether its contents lead you to want
to explore further or simply enable you to know that this
college should be crossed off your list.

Brochures are especially important in the case of small
liberal arts colleges, some of which are superb but virtually
unknown. Others are worthless and unknown, so that sorting them out will take some detective work.

Some of the numbers in brochures can be tricky. Student-faculty ratios from large universities may not mean
the same thing as student-faculty ratios from small colleges. At a university with hundreds of graduate teaching
assistants, many part-time junior faculty, and many senior
faculty with research grants that reduce the number of
courses they teach, much depends on how they choose to
define and count "faculty." In more than a decade on the

faculty of U.C.L.A., I actually taught courses only about five years, spent nearly four years living in Palo Alto (400 miles away), and more than two years living on the east coast—all the while being counted as part of the faculty of U.C.L.A. This is not that unusual at a large research university, where senior faculty are often on leave for extended periods of time. Moreover, even when they are on campus, many senior faculty at such institutions spend most of their time with graduate students.

Student-faculty ratios may be useful if you don't take them too literally, and if you compare liberal arts colleges with one another rather than with large universities. For all institutions, this ratio gives only a rough idea of average class size. If one university has a 30-to-1 ratio and another has a 15-to-1 ratio, then the first probably has bigger classes. But if one university has a 20-to-1 ratio and another has 18-to-1, it may simply mean that they are defining "faculty" differently, or counting full-time and part-time students or faculty differently.

There are other statistical traps to avoid when trying to determine whether you will be lost in a mob or receive individual attention in class. If, at 10 o'clock on a Monday morning, there are a thousand students in class, with half of them in a huge lecture hall holding 500 students, then half the students have mass, impersonal education. The other half may be scattered in 20 other classes, getting more individual attention. If this pattern is typical throughout the week, then the human reality is that half the time you are likely to be getting mass education at that college. What its brochure will say, however, is that the average class size is less than 25. It will be correct—but misleading. Merely by changing the focus from the student's experience as the unit of observation to the classroom as the unit of observation, the brochure has changed the meaning and relevance of its statistics.

Harvard's brochure shows that it has more than 500 courses with 20 or fewer students, and less than 70 courses with 100 or more students. The temptation is to say that there are more Harvard students taking small classes—and the brochure's presentation leads you in that direction—but you cannot simply compare the number of small classes with the number of large classes. By definition, there are more people in each large class, so that an unweighted average would be invalid and misleading. Judging by the distribution of class sizes, there are probably at least as many Harvard students taking classes with 100 or more students as are taking classes with 20 or less. (To illustrate the mathematical principle involved with a deliberately extravagant example, if there were a million students in one college, with 900,000 of them enrolled in one course and the other 100,000 in one-person tutorials, then the average class size would be 10, even though 90 percent of the students were in a class larger than the population of San Francisco.) There is a fundamental difference between making the student the focus and making the classroom the focus.

✔ CATALOGUES

College catalogues are usually less flashy and more factual than brochures. They are also usually a little harder to obtain, but they can be gotten if you are persistent. Many schools will send the brochure if you write and ask for a catalogue. In this case, it would be advisable to phone the admissions office and explain that you specifically want the catalogue. Some colleges, such as Harvard, Chicago, and U.C.L.A., charge you for the catalogue, but five dollars usually covers it, so that is not a major problem. For a university with many divisions, it would be necessary to specify whether the catalogue you wanted was for the undergraduate liberal arts college, the college of engineering, or whatever other division you were interested in.

Because the catalogue has more facts and less fluff than the brochure, it is something to turn to after you have already narrowed down your choices to perhaps 5 or 10 schools and plan to look at each in depth. The main body of most catalogues consists of a listing of courses, each with a description of what is covered. It is seldom worthwhile to read very many of these course descriptions but sometimes a knowledgeable person can tell whether the collection of offerings in a given department makes sense. A mathematician looking at a list of courses in a math department, or a chemist looking at the courses in a chemistry department, can tell if what is offered is adequate or inadequate as a foundation in that field. In some colleges, taking everything that is offered in a given department will still not be enough, even if the courses are all well taught and you master all the material in them.

If you don't know any chemist or mathematician, your high school chemistry or mathematics teacher may be willing to look at some catalogue listings in chemistry or math for you. To keep your request reasonable, you should not inundate your teacher with catalogues but seek his or her opinion only after you have narrowed your college choices down to the final few. You may also mention that you don't expect the teacher to know what the actual quality of the courses is, but only to tell you if some set of department offerings is inadequate to cover the field properly. In other words, you are not asking for a definitive evaluation but only for help in weeding out something that should not be considered any further. However, it may turn out in some cases that the teacher does have some idea of the quality of a particular department. If so, that is a windfall gain.

Another very important piece of information in most college catalogues concerns the academic background of the faculty. Again, this is something to look up only after you have reduced your list of colleges to the final few. Most catalogues list the faculty, their degrees, and their academic rank, usually toward the back. Sometimes, merely going through the list and underlining the universities from which they received their Ph.D.'s will show differences that provide important clues when choosing a college.

Bennington College, which has had the distinction of being the most expensive college in the country, is notable for the relatively low percentage of Ph.D.'s among its faculty. Partly this is because such a high proportion of the Bennington faculty specializes in areas such as painting, ceramics, music, and dance, in which Ph.D.'s are not the relevant training. Among those Bennington professors with Ph.D.'s, some are from top-ranked universities, such as Harvard, Chicago, and Berkeley. Still, even in traditional subjects such as literature, history, and mathematics, there are more faculty members without doctorates than you would expect from a college with such expensive tuition.

Although Bennington faculty list their publications in the catalogue (very unusual), publications in respected scholarly journals are conspicuous by their absence. No one expects professors at a liberal arts college to match the volume of scholarly publications found among professors at a research university. But the *quality* of what is published by professors at a top-ranked liberal arts college is often good enough to be published in the leading professional journals in their fields. It is worth noting that this does not seem to be true for most Bennington faculty.

Bennington has long been known for marching to its own drummer, and this unusual assortment of faculty is in keeping with that pattern. The question here is not whether this is good or bad, but whether it suits what you are looking for. Whether it is or not, a careful reading of the faculty's credentials gives you some important clues—not only at Bennington, but in general.

Sometimes a casual look through the faculty listings will be enough to turn up significant differences in the educational backgrounds of professors at different colleges. Swarthmore College professors, for example, tend to have Ph.D.'s overwhelmingly from the very top-ranked universities, while those at Whittier College have Ph.D.'s from a more mixed assortment of top-tier and second-tier universities—very good on the whole, but not a match for Swarthmore. When comparing any colleges in this respect, the educational backgrounds of professors of music, art, physical education, and the like should not be included in comparisons with professors in academic fields where the Ph.D. is the norm.

Much controversy has swirled around the Ph.D. degree—whether it is crucial, whether it matters where it came from, and many other issues. Like test scores, its significance can be readily contested in individual cases. There have been a few leading scholars with no Ph.D., or with Ph.D.'s from some institution of secondary rank. But it is rare. If you look at any list of professors who have reached special prominence in their fields—presidents of the American Economic Association, for example—you will find that virtually all received their post-graduate education at one of a relatively small number of highly rated universities. By the time professors reach such a level of eminence, most people have long ago forgotten where their Ph.D.'s came from, so that it is their achievements which are being recognized by their professional colleagues. That only makes this "coincidence" all the more striking.

No one should imagine that a college where 90 percent of the faculty have Ph.D.'s is automatically superior to a college where 85 percent of the faculty have Ph.D.'s, or that every professor with a Ph.D. from Ohio State is less qualified than every professor with a Ph.D. from Yale. Everyone knows that a second-baseman on a team that won the World Series isn't necessarily better than all other second-basemen, and similar reasoning applies here to individual professors. But you are not choosing individual professors until you have already chosen a college—and the college has chosen you. Right now, you are choosing a team—a faculty—and the point here is that a World Championship team is usually better than a team that didn't make the playoffs.

Choosing a college is a question of making some general assessments and seeing if they add up to a decisive difference. Often they won't, but where they do, it can be very important. Pettifogging arguments should not be allowed to stand in the way of making general assessments where the differences are large. It may not matter that 90 percent of college A's faculty have Ph.D.'s compared to 85 percent of college B's faculty, but if only 50 percent of college C's faculty have Ph.D.'s, then a real question arises. There may be a good answer to that question—but there had better be.

If you are particularly interested in the professors who teach some special field that you plan to major in, it might be well worth finding out how the departments from which they received their Ph.D.'s are ranked by those in that profession. The National Academy of Sciences publishes such rankings, and they do not always conform to the general prestige of the universities in which the departments are located. For example, most people would probably rank Cornell or Yale over the University of California at Davis, but U.C. Davis is ranked number one in the country in botany by those in that field (with Cornell 5th and Yale 7th), so a professor of botany with a Ph.D. from Davis is the top of the line as far as his professional training is concerned. Similarly, the University of Houston is ranked above Princeton in chemical engineering.

Here we are now doing something that we avoided doing before: ranking institutions by their academic quality. But we are doing so only in a limited sense—*after* reaching the point where you have already determined the range of your own academic capabilities, the kind of institutional atmosphere you are seeking, and many other personal considerations. Within that range of desired characteristics, it is obviously better being taught by better-qualified professors.

Many feel that it is not the professor's own educational background or scholarly achievements that matter most, but how good he or she is in the classroom. However, as we saw in Chapter 3, there are important aspects of teaching that cannot be determined by observation in the classroom. Research at Harvard showed that how much was actually learned by students in introductory economics there had no correlation with how high the students rated their teacher—but *was* correlated with their teacher's grades in graduate school. My own experience likewise suggests that, in general, it is the quality and capability of the professor's mind—more than anything else—that determines how much the students learn, not whether they enjoy the process or are impressed by him or her. I encountered an extreme example of this while teaching at Howard University in Washington.

In an upper-level economics course called "intermediate price theory," I found some of my Howard students following the work very intelligently while a surprising number of others obviously didn't have a clue as to what I was talking about. During informal discussions with individual students in my office, I would casually ask who had taught them introductory economics. Some mentioned Professor A, usually with warm comments on what a good teacher he was. These were almost invariably students who were totally lost in intermediate price theory and failing the course. Professor A had simply never given them the essential foundation for further study of economics. How could the students possibly have known this while enjoying whatever it was that he did teach?

On the other hand, there were other students in the course who had been taught introductory economics by Professor Z, a no-nonsense man with an accent that some found hard to understand. Students complained, often bitterly, about him as a teacher. But everyone who had a grade of B or above at that point in intermediate price theory had been taught introductory economics by Professor Z. Given what they had learned in his course, they had no trouble picking up the story and continuing on in mine, without missing a beat. One professor had impressed them; the other had taught them.

Variations on this episode have occurred at other colleges and universities where I have taught. At Douglass College, the women's college at Rutgers University, I was hired to fill a vacancy caused by a retiring professor who was so revered by some students that I made it a point never to say anything to suggest that I was *replacing* him. But I soon discovered that students who had studied economics under him were usually not only lacking in preparation for upper-level work, but often had a complete misconception of what economics was all about. I discouraged his former students from taking my courses until after they had taken an economic theory course taught by one of my colleagues—even though I admitted other students who had had no economics at all. It was easier to give special help to students who didn't know anything about the subject than to try to unscramble somebody who had been confused by my highly regarded predecessor.

In short, while irresponsibility, disorganization, and sheer propaganda by a professor may be detected by students in the classroom, the positive things—what makes it all meaningful and worthwhile—cannot be assessed for a college faculty in general without some external clues as to their educational preparation and capabilities, as judged by those professionally qualified to judge.

✔ FINANCIAL WEEDING

Colleges have to be weeded out financially, as well as academically, socially, and in other ways. Some students may see the big question as whether they can afford to go to college at all, not where. Certainly that was the way the problem once presented itself to me, and to many others of my generation. Today, that is much less of a problem because so much more financial aid is available. Whether you can go, from a financial point of view, is often more of a question of living expenses rather than tuition. It is also a question of whether you or your family can afford to have you pass up a full-time paycheck in order to study. No one can answer this last question for you, especially if you have other people dependent on you. But if you are single and free of dependents, and don't mind postponing full-time paychecks, the opportunities are large.

Horrendous tuitions are often reported in the media. Many colleges charge more than $10,000 a year, not counting room and board. However, those tuitions are often like list prices on cars or other products that are almost always sold at a discount. In the academic world, that discount is called "financial aid."

In general, the more expensive the tuition, the fewer the students who pay it in full, or at all. This is true not only at the rich-and-famous institutions like Harvard, Chicago, or Stanford, but much more broadly. Approximately 70 percent of the students at Birmingham-Southern College receive some form of financial aid, whether as an outright grant or as a loan, a campus job, or (more likely) some combination. The same is true at the University of Puget Sound, where the average financial aid is about the same as at Harvard. At Tulane University, the average financial aid is even greater than at Harvard.

Financial aid may of course go beyond tuition to cover all or part of your living expenses. Nor do you need to be from a low-income family to qualify, though in general the likelihood of receiving larger awards tends to be greater for students from moderate- to low-income families. Still, it is not at all uncommon for students whose families earn $50,000 or more to receive some financial aid. Again, this practice is not confined to rich Ivy League schools. At Knox College, for example, the great majority of those students from families making over $50,000 a year who applied for financial aid received it. The average amount of the aid was not as large as for those from families with lower incomes, but still it ranged up to several thousand dollars a year. Moreover, *all* of those students from families earning less than $42,000 a year who applied for financial aid received it, some in amounts exceeding tuition by enough to cover a substantial part of living expenses.

A similar pattern can be found at Carleton College, among others. In the academic year 1985–1986, for example, there were 51 freshmen whose family incomes were $60,000 and over who nevertheless "demonstrated need" by the college's criteria and were awarded financial aid averaging more than $4,000 per year. The same was true for all in lower income brackets, with the amount of the aid increasing until it exceeded $10,000 per year for students whose annual family income was below $12,000. None of these institutions is unique. Their statistics are cited simply to illustrate a more widespread pattern.

Just as there are nationwide organizations for administering college entrance tests and forwarding the results to individual institutions, so there are nationwide organizations to assess your financial aid needs and forward those results to individual colleges. There is a standard *Financial Aid Form* to be filled out and forwarded to the College Scholarship Service in Princeton or a *Family Financial Statement* to be filed with the American College Testing Program in Iowa City. These should be available in your high school but, if not, you can write to get them from either of these organizations. Their addresses are:

> Educational Testing Service
> College Scholarship Service
> CN 6300
> Princeton, New Jersey 08541

American College Testing Program
Family Financial Statement
P.O. Box 1002
Iowa City, Iowa 52243

Applying for financial aid involves more than filling out another set of forms. It also involves another set of application deadlines—often *earlier* than the deadline for admissions applications. If financial aid is essential for you to go to college, the earlier financial aid deadline is the one that counts. It might be an especially bitter disappointment to be admitted to the college of your choice and then not be able to go because you didn't complete the financial aid forms in time.

Despite the generous financial aid available at many colleges, not everyone can gain admission to these colleges. If you have gone through high school with a C average and your verbal and math S.A.T.'s are each in the 400's, then you cannot assume that you will be admitted to places like Knox College or Birmingham-Southern, much less to big-name colleges and universities, where admissions applications exceed the number of available places by several times over. Nevertheless, most states have a sufficiently wide range of state colleges, state universities, and community colleges that you should be able to find a niche somewhere. If you are from New Hampshire and can't get into the University of New Hampshire, then you may be able to get into Keene State College. If you are from Texas and can't get admitted to the Austin campus of the University of Texas, your chances may be better at the El Paso campus. In California, there is an even wider spectrum of state institutions, headed by Berkeley and U.C.L.A. in terms of prestige (and by U.C. San Diego in terms of your chances of continuing on to the doctorate).

Financial aid may not be as generous in all parts of the academic pecking order, but it is available in most, through a wide variety of state and federal programs too numerous to list. High school counselors or college admission officers should be able to direct you to whatever financial aid programs are best suited to your situation. But, whatever others may invest in your education, the largest investment will still be your own. Four years of passing up full-time paychecks adds up to a lot of money—far more than any loans you are likely to get. Throw in the element of chance—that you may not graduate, after all, or may not find a well-paying career if you do—and the prospect may require a lot of sober thought, especially if your academic performance and academic interest are marginal. For those who are determined, such considerations will not stop them—and may spur them on to work harder, to make sure their investment (or gamble) pays off.

Co-operative work-study programs may be of special interest to those with financial concerns, or those who are anxious to sample some profession while in college, before deciding whether to make it their life's work. Kalamazoo College's program, mentioned earlier, is only one of many. Co-op programs are found at all academic quality levels, in all geographic regions, and from huge universities to small liberal arts colleges and at a number of engineering schools.

Sometimes these work-study programs are available only in particular fields (engineering at Arizona State University or the University of Florida, chemistry at Butler University). Sometimes they cover a variety of fields, as they do at Ohio State or the University of Virginia. Finally, there are schools like Kalamazoo, Northeastern, and Drexel, where the whole academic program is built around co-operative work-study programs. Whether at specialized co-op institutions or at other colleges, universities, or engineering schools, work-study programs may delay graduation, perhaps by a year—but they need not. It does not at Kalamazoo, for example. This will have to be checked out at each institution.

One of the trade-offs involved in work-study programs is the frequent disruption of collegiate life and perhaps the loss of summer vacations. When one semester is spent on campus and the next semester working hundreds of miles away, continuity of friendships with classmates will be harder to maintain. Those who treasure a collegiate experience of fraternities, football games, and the like, will also find that the demands of co-operative work-study put a real damper on such things. In short, it is not for everybody. But that is true of many worthwhile things.

No discussion of finances should leave out those rare institutions with no tuition at all. Aside from military service academies like West Point and Annapolis, there is Berea College in Kentucky, where everyone works at least 10 hours a week—and where you can be rejected for admission if your family income is too high. It also has a policy of taking most of its students from the Appalachian region. A very small, elite, and avant-garde two-year college in California called Deep Springs likewise has no tuition and has student work requirements.

The final piece of financial weeding-out may come when you are accepted at more than one college and have to decide not only how one institution compares to another but also how one financial aid package compares to another. That happy problem will be left for the last chapter.

CHAPTER 10

THE CAMPUS VISIT

Most colleges have regular programs of campus visits by prospective students. Often they can find a place in a dormitory for a visiting student and a place in some classes that students and parents wish to sit in on. These visits can tell you things that no amount of reading can.

When you hear stereos blasting away in the dorms on past midnight, that carries its own unmistakable message. When the food tastes so bad you can't eat it, no one needs to say anything. When graffiti defaces the buildings, inside and out, you get a clue as to what kind of people you are dealing with.

Not all clues you pick up on campus visits are bad. When I walked all over the campus at Whitman College and at Franklin & Marshall without discovering a single bit of graffiti, that told me something positive about the attitudes and behavior of the students. When I saw valuable possessions left outdoors unguarded at Harvey Mudd College, that was also an encouraging sign. Just walking around campus asking directions, and finding helpfulness at every turn, told me something about the University of Evansville. These are all small things, but they add up—and sometimes, when the campus visit is over and you consider them all, they add up to a pretty clear picture, one way or the other.

Like anything else, a campus visit will be more productive the better it is planned. Make reservations weeks in advance and make a list before you get there, so that you will know what you want to check out. That list should include: the dormitories, the food, the classes, safety, the library, the bookstore, and—most important of all—the people. Parents will probably notice different things than a student will notice, and miss some things that a student will see. That is all to the good because, between you, you will cover a wider range of things than either would have covered alone.

Whatever you notice, *write it down*. Months can pass between a campus visit and the decision to apply—and more months between the application and your receipt of acceptance letters, which is when you must make the most important decision. Do not expect every memory to survive all that time, much less to survive accurately. If you visit several campuses, memories may start to run together, leaving you uncertain as to what happened where. Worse, you may remember incidents on one campus as happening on another. Write it down when it happens.

✔ PROFESSORS

It is usually easy to see college admissions officials during a campus visit and it may be easy to strike up conversations with students or with people in town, but getting to see the professors is much harder on some campuses. At some large research universities, you may get no closer to a big-name professor than his secretary's office. This is not just because you are a visitor; his own students may have the same problem.

This too differs greatly from one college to another. On some campuses, most professors have their office doors open and will not mind at all if you stop in for a couple of questions or to ask for a copy of a syllabus. A campus visit is the best way—perhaps the only way—to find out what faculty attitudes and availability are like at a college you are considering.

For someone choosing a college, the most important thing about a professor is his teaching. While you cannot just intrude into a classroom where you have not been invited, often the admissions office can find some professors who don't mind having visitors. Try to arrange this before you arrive for the visit—or at least early on the first day, if you are going to be on campus more than one day.

When you go to a professor's lecture, take a checklist with you, rather than rely on general impressions written down afterwards—or, worse yet, rely on memory. The checklist should include simple things that you should be able to expect from any professor, but cannot:

1. Does the professor arrive on time?
2. Does the lecture begin promptly?
3. Is the lecture well organized or rambling?
4. Are questions from the students welcomed? Answered clearly?
5. Are students who disagree with the professor treated with respect or put down?
6. Is the professor available after the lecture is over for informal discussions with students who have further questions or comments?

You may not be able to answer every question on your checklist for every professor, but the answers you are able to write down can still be very valuable—especially if they fall into a clear pattern at one college and a very different pattern at another.

At some large research universities, a big-name professor may think nothing of showing up late for class, and after the lecture may exit so quickly that a student sitting in the back of the room would have to be an Olympic sprinter to catch him before he has escaped to his office or the parking lot. Not all are like this by any means. But if your campus visits include a major research university, try to sit in on the lectures of some senior professors. Sometimes the younger faculty members have not yet developed the same arrogance, or dare not show it yet. In any case, see for yourself.

While attending lectures will not enable you to make a complete assessment of the teaching, for reasons already discussed in Chapters 5 and 9, it can give you good, first-hand information on some important aspects of teaching. It will add to the accumulation of information from various sources, which in the end can add up to enough to make it much easier to choose a college. One of the other items you should try to add to your collection are some syllabuses from courses at each college you visit.

The syllabus in some subject like mathematics may contain little more than the name of the textbook and a list of pages to read and problems to do on given dates. For some "social science" courses, however, there may be a large number of readings from various sources. You may not be able to evaluate these, but perhaps you will know someone who can. Even in a more or less cut-and-dried course like introductory calculus, a high school math teacher may be able to tell you whether the textbook used is appropriate for that level or is too easy or too hard. In social science courses where differences of opinions and viewpoints come in, someone who knows the subject can tell you whether there is some attempt at balance in the syllabus or whether it is so lopsided as to be propaganda rather than education.

Where there is only one textbook used in the course, then it matters greatly whether that textbook presents a balanced interpretation. For example, if an American history course uses as its textbook *A People's History of the United States* by Howard Zinn, then you know that the course is not only propaganda but crude propaganda at that. *Pravda*'s attacks on the United States are more subtle than Zinn's. It is not the textbook writer's politics but the book's own quality that is at issue. Another history textbook, on slavery, is *Roll, Jordan, Roll* by Marxist professor Eugene Genovese but it is a real work of scholarship and perhaps the best book on the subject.

If you miss an opportunity to get the syllabuses you want during a campus visit, you can write for them after you get back home. Most professors will probably be glad to send you one. You can usually get the name of the professor teaching a particular course from the college catalogue. If not, the catalogue will probably list the department chairman, and the chairman can pass the request along to the right person.

Not all of these syllabuses will give you significant clues. But if some do, then you are that much ahead, and it hasn't cost much money or time. Because Howard Zinn's book is so bad that it makes a good litmus test of what a course is trying to do, you may want to ask for a syllabus for the American history course on each campus.

You may discover positive as well as negative things

from a syllabus. If it's a course on social philosophy that assigns both John Rawls and Robert Nozick, then you know that the professor wants you to deal with opposing viewpoints, not just buy some party line. The same is true if it is an economics course that assigns both John Kenneth Galbraith and Milton Friedman, or a course on Constitutional law that assigns such scholars on one side as Laurence Tribe or Ronald Dworkin, and on the other side such scholars as Richard Posner or Robert Bork. There are still professors who honor the old adage: "We are here to teach you *how* to think, not *what* to think."

✔ DORMITORIES

Dormitories seldom look impressive, either for architecture or neatness. But if the dormitories on the campus you visit have halls that look like a pigsty and the place strikes you as a firetrap, you need to make a note of it. If it is possible to have an overnight stay, this will be the best indicator of all. A student left alone will quickly discover whether it is easy or hard to meet people, as well as whether it is quiet enough to study or quiet enough to sleep. There are also things that young people can talk about together much more freely when parents are not around. Depending on what you are looking for and what the college has to offer, the overnight stay can make or break your decision to apply.

As noted in Chapter 6, some co-ed dorms are more co-ed than others. When young people are talking without the older generation around, it shouldn't be hard to find out about this, as well as about the availability of drugs and alcohol and how prevalent is their use. Even with all due allowance for the fact that one night is just one night, and may not be typical, some things will tell you all you want to know—or more than you want to know.

✔ THE LOCAL COMMUNITY

Parents may be staying in a motel near the campus while the student is spending the night in the dorms, but they can also be busy, gathering information about the town and its people. Just walking around a little and keeping your eyes and ears open will often turn up a few interesting indicators of what the community is like. If the streets near the college are full of bookstores, coffee shops, bicycle stores, and pizza parlors, that is a very different scene from a college ringed around with porno shops and shady characters dealing drugs on the streets. If all the clothing stores near the campus sell things that are way beyond your budget, you may want to think about whether you have gotten in with a country club crowd, which might be uncomfortable socially as well as financially. As with other aspects of a college, minor differences don't matter but big differences can.

If parents take each meal at a different restaurant in town, and chat with waitressess or cashiers at each, they are bound to pick up more impressions or clues from more people. It may also be well worth the price of a bottle of aspirin and a couple of postcards to stop by the local drugstore and chat with the people who run it. If you are driving, filling up the car in town will provide yet another occasion to talk with someone local and unofficial. Just turning the radio dial can sometimes give you a clue, especially if all you can get is bluegrass music and reports on hog prices.

If you are really into bluegrass music and hog prices, you may have found Utopia. If not, then you are sadder but wiser.

It may be useful not only to pick up a copy of the student newspaper and the local community newspaper while you are visiting, but also to buy a subscription as well. A month's subscription to each will probably tell you all you need to know, but some college newspapers can only be subscribed to for a semester, a quarter, or an academic year. However, that should not be a deterrent, as the cost is usually modest. The *Harvard Crimson* is one of the most expensive student newspapers, because it can only be subscribed to for a full academic year, but even so the cost is less than 50 dollars. Other student newspaper subscriptions cost less than half of that. If you are visiting half a dozen campuses, you may be able to subscribe to the student newspaper at each college for a total cost of less than 100 dollars. That is a bargain for information about an investment that can run into tens of thousands of dollars and four years of your life. It is not necessary to read every issue of each newspaper from cover to cover. A quick glance may tell you whether there is anything salient in an issue and if you get three significant clues in a month, you will have gotten your money's worth. You can seldom buy valuable information about such a big investment for such little money.

One of the things you can learn about from local and campus newspapers—and other sources—is safety. If the biggest crime news in a month is the theft of a bicycle that was left outdoors and unlocked overnight, that tells you something—something welcome, in this case. This may in fact be the biggest crime news in some small college towns. The student newspaper at the University of Chicago, *The*

Maroon, regularly publishes official crime statistics for the area. *The Trail*, the student newspaper at the University of Puget Sound, covers crimes specifically on campus. Other college papers report only serious or unusual crimes. Sometimes you can get an impression of safety by noticing stores in town after they have closed. If a photography store leaves expensive cameras sitting exposed behind a plate glass window, it is probably because the danger of theft is not worth the cost of an iron grate or the bother of putting the cameras away every night.

With something as important as safety, you do not want to rely solely on casual observations, however. Ask questions at the college. Is there an organized escort service for young women coming home late at night from the library or from social events? Does anyone use it, if it is available— or do they feel secure enough that it isn't worth the bother? Does the campus security officer have any idea (or statistics) on campus crime? Talk with him and find out. If the college publishes a pamphlet of safety tips, you should get one and take it with you. It is something to keep, not only until you decide where to apply, but also until admissions decisions have been made and you have to choose among the colleges that accepted you.

For a more detailed statistical profile of the local community, you may even want to purchase a copy of a Census publication called *County and City Data Book*, which gives everything from the local crime rate to the ethnic, economic, and educational breakdowns of the local population. This may seem like an awful lot to go into, and it would certainly be far too much at an earlier stage of the weeding-out process. But, by the time of the campus visit, your list of colleges should be down to a half dozen or so. It may be worth putting these few under a microscope, especially if you like the college but have some real questions that trouble you about its location.

Looking into the local community does not imply that a student is expected to spend a lot of time there. The local community may be important primarily in terms of safety and negative influences in general. Its other features may be of limited relevance, especially at colleges with heavy and demanding work loads. Studying into the wee hours of the morning in New Brunswick, New Jersey, is not very different from studying into the wee hours of the morning in Chicago or Honolulu. Most social life at many colleges is centered on campus. Those students with especially wide cultural horizons may be concerned about being near a major symphony orchestra, art museum, ski resorts, discos, and the opera. But such people will have no problem checking such things out. Most others will find that there is far more going on, on campus, than they can keep up with—even if the campus itself is located in the middle of nowhere.

Local community newspapers and student newspapers that you have subscribed to will continue to add to your knowledge of the cultural scene at the college and in town after your campus visit is over. This will not only give a picture of the amount and kind of entertainment available, but also may provide clues about the diversity of speakers and the tolerance or intolerance on campus. If Jane Fonda speaks one month and Milton Friedman the next, then that is a hopeful sign, especially if both speak without disruption. During your visit, the college public affairs office may be able to supply a list of the previous speakers on campus. Ask to see it. Take a copy with you if you can or write down the names if you can't. Even if some (or all) of the names mean nothing to you, your family, friends, teachers, or classmates may be able to identify enough of them, after you return from the visit, to enable you to form a picture.

✔ LIBRARIES

After you have gone around and seen a few colleges, their libraries—like other campus features—may start to look like they are all the same. But they are enormously different if you know what to look for, and these differences can sometimes tell you a lot about differences in the schools, the students, and the quality of the education.

One of the most important things about a library can usually be found on the front door: the hours the library is open. Write them down in a notebook during your campus visit. When the library at one college closes at 5 P.M. on weekends, while the library at another college remains open past midnight on weekends, that gives you a clue. When you walk around inside a library and notice whether the students are quietly sitting down poring over their books or mostly standing around talking and checking out the opposite sex, that's another clue.

The time of day when you look at a library can make a difference. If you show up at the library when it first opens up in the morning, on some campuses you will see a crowd of students already gathered outside, waiting to get in, while on other campuses only a handful of hardy souls will enter the library during the first hour it is open. Some college libraries are almost deserted on a Friday night or a Saturday afternoon. At other colleges, the library remains packed as long as the doors are open.

No single clue by itself is all-important. Moreover, you have to make allowances for the fact that your campus visit may be just before exams at one school and right after exams at another. But, even when all due allowances are made, often the clues picked up at the library all point in the same direction and dovetail with clues picked up elsewhere on campus and in town. Keeping a notebook on your observations at each college will make it easier to see a pattern in all these separate items and to compare colleges after you return home.

If you are fortunate enough to have parents who are professionals in some field—if your father is a chemist or your mother is a sociologist—then they can check out whether the library has the leading or latest books in their specialties. Probably it will, but if the library lacks the books and scholarly journals that a well-informed faculty would need, chances are that the faculty is not as well informed (or as interested in keeping well informed) as it should be. They may be fine teachers, in the sense of classroom performance, but what they teach may be out of date.

Libraries are an integral part of the teaching process—or should be—and large disparities between libraries on different campuses are often indicative of differences in the whole approach to education. Where mass-production education reigns, reading assignments are likely to be concentrated in textbooks that the students buy, thereby requiring relatively little use of the library. Where the education provides more diverse viewpoints and is enriched with articles from scholarly journals, or teaches the history of ideas from original sources rather than textbook summaries, all this means much heavier use of the library and requires far larger library resources in proportion to the student body.

In this context, the number of books in a library is not just a dry statistic, though it must be assessed in terms of the number of students on campus. For example, the library at the University of Chicago has only about 37 percent more books than the library at Ohio State University in Columbus. This would not be a very important difference by itself. However, when you realize that Ohio State has more than five times as many students as the University of Chicago, the real disparity becomes much greater. There are more than *seven times as many books per student* at Chicago. Even allowing for the fact that most students at Chicago are post-graduate students, while most of those at Ohio State are undergraduates, the disparity is still so huge as to tell you something about the differences in education at the two institutions.

As with other academic indicators, such as S.A.T. scores or faculty Ph.D.'s, small statistical differences in libraries do not necessarily mean anything—but vast differences raise questions, at the very least. Such indicators are especially valuable when comparing colleges you have not known of before. You may never have heard of either Goucher College or Grove City College, but when you learn that the library at Goucher has twice as many books for half as many students, you have at least one clue as to the differences between the two schools.

The whole content of college courses can be strongly influenced by the limitations of the library. My reading lists for courses I taught at Cornell, Amherst, and Douglass College contained far more "outside readings" than my reading lists for the same courses when I taught them at U.C.L.A. In turn, this meant that classroom discussions at U.C.L.A. were more limited and that some important and challenging topics could only be summarized in lectures rather than being explored by students in class discussions, in a way that would have produced a deeper understanding.

Although U.C.L.A. has the largest library collection of these four institutions, its huge undergraduate population and bureaucratic regulations had the net effect of watering down those courses where supplementary readings would have been especially valuable. The U.C.L.A. research library is superb—which is fine for professors and graduate students—but the library handling reserved readings for undergraduates could not compare in quality to libraries serving much smaller student bodies at Amherst, Cornell, or Douglass College.

As in other areas involving statistics, numbers make good servants but bad masters. They cannot be followed blindly without regard to what is being compared. Not only must library resources be related to the number of students they serve; comparisons between libraries at engineering schools and libraries at liberal arts colleges must be avoided, along with other pitfalls. The best comparisons are between similar institutions: two liberal arts colleges or two research universities, for example.

The vast library holdings at the U.C.L.A. law school or the Harvard Business School do little for an undergraduate at these institutions. At Rutgers University, the library for the whole system—stretching from Camden (near Philadelphia) to Newark (near New York)—contains 3.8 million volumes. But it is very misleading to list 3.8 million volumes as the library holdings at Douglass College, as Cass and Birnbaum's *Comparative Guide to American Colleges* does. All these books are available to Douglass College students in some theoretical sense, but they are by no means in the library on their campus. Nor are they on any one of the other Rutgers University campuses for which the same 3.8 million volumes are listed as their library holdings.

When you reach the point where you have only a handful

of colleges left to consider, if you want to compare institutions which have multiple libraries for multiple purposes,
your best bet may be to seek data on the volumes in their
undergraduate liberal arts college library on one campus.
Even this provides only a rough indicator, but it will probably be less misleading than statistics on university-wide
library holdings, especially for a multiple-campus university. The campus visit is a good time to get such information
but of course you can also phone or write for it.

✔ BOOKSTORES

Like libraries, college bookstores may also have a few
useful clues to offer during a campus visit. In some college
bookstores, the only serious books are the textbooks assigned for courses. If the rest of the books are few and
fluffy, it is probably because neither students nor faculty
have much demand for anything beyond that. If it's all Dan-
ielle Steel and coffee-table books once you get out of the
textbook section, this may tell you something.

Again, you have to make allowances. If there is a mam-
moth private bookstore across the street doing a land-office
business in heavyweight reading, the college store may decide that it can just stick to textbooks. One of the most
magnificent bookstores you can find is located in South Had-
ley, Massachusetts, near Mount Holyoke College. What the
college bookstore has may be much less of an indicator of
student and faculty intellectual interests there than it
would be otherwise. However, nothing of this sort can explain the meager offerings of the college bookstore at Willamette University in Salem, Oregon, or at Muhlenberg
College in Allentown, Pennsylvania.

✔ FOOD

No college visit is complete without sampling the food on campus. This is unlikely to be the high point of the visit but it is a very necessary evil. College food is seldom *haute cuisine* but there are significant differences between mediocre, edible, and swill. These differences can translate into substantial differences in the cost of an education, if students are frequently driven to buy meals at local fast-food restaurants and pizza parlors, despite having been forced to pay in advance for the college meal plan.

Despite the desirability of a list of colleges whose food is excellent, my 30 years of visiting campuses across the United States and around the world have left few memories of outstanding food, even in the faculty clubs. Perhaps you may find some. The more urgent practical task, however, is to distinguish the mediocre from the truly awful. At Willamette University, for example, I sat down to lunch hungry from having skipped breakfast, but ended up consuming only a glass of milk and the crackers that came with the soup. There was no way I was going to eat the soup itself, the sandwich, or even the dessert. Still, it was a valuable experience and saved me the cost of an application fee. That is the spirit in which eating on campus should be approached during a campus visit. As a visitor, you can always leave the food alone after you have checked it out, and go eat in a restaurant in town. But four years of doing that can be very expensive.

If the food doesn't pass muster but the college is good otherwise, see if the meal plan is optional or mandatory. If the meal plan is optional, the next order of business is to check out the local alternatives for quality and cost. At some colleges and universities, the campus is the only game in town, as far as affordable meals are concerned. At other places, there are wholesome meals available off campus at reasonable prices or there may be cooking facilities for the students in the dormitories. Seldom, however, are any of these alternatives as desirable as having good food already prepared for you, so that your time is free for taking care of the business of getting an education, rather than being used up shopping at supermarkets, cooking, and washing dishes.

In judging food, it is worth remembering that the kind of food you can put up with for one day during a visit is not necessarily the kind of food you could eat all year long. If not, then taking breaks from the campus food can easily add hundreds of dollars to the annual college cost.

CHAPTER 11

THE ADMISSIONS GAME

The first thing to recognize about the admissions game is that it is a game. It has a large element of chance, as well as much strategy and counter-strategy between college applicants and admissions officials. The admissions game has its rules but its outcome is often much like the erratic bounce of a football, which can make all the difference between a touchdown for you and a touchdown for the other team. There have been experiments done where the same set of credentials was submitted to the same college under two different names, with one being accepted and the other rejected. If admissions decisions were computerized, this would not happen but human beings on an admissions committee cannot keep all the applicants in mind simultaneously or rank them all against one another.

In any game, you first need to know the rules and then know the other players. Only then can you plan strategy.

✔ RULES OF THE GAME

There are different versions of the admissions game, each with its own rules, and the popularity of each version varies from place to place and from time to time. The most straightforward rule is that whoever meets the requirements gets admitted. For colleges, universities, and engineering schools with this kind of rule, your main concern may be to make sure that you meet the requirements. But, even here, it gets more complicated.

Just as you are playing the game for your benefit, so institutions are playing the game for their benefit. Many state universities know that the more students they admit—the more warm bodies they have on campus—the more money they can get out of state legislators. Their admissions standards may therefore be set low enough to ensure that they always have enough warm bodies on campus, even if many of those admitted do not survive the freshman year.

It is not at all uncommon for 30 or 40 percent of the freshman class to fail to make it through to the sophomore year at some state universities. Barely half the entering freshmen have graduated five years later at the University of Texas at Austin, the University of Vermont at Burlington, the University of Wisconsin at Madison, or the University of California at Santa Barbara. *Less* than half have graduated in five years at the University of Washington at Seattle or the University of California at Santa Cruz, Riverside, or Irvine. These are by no means the worst, or even exceptional, though there are other state institutions like the University of Virginia, William & Mary, or New College, where the survival rates are much higher.

With state universities, another factor that enters into the admissions decision is whether the applicant is from within the state or not. At the University of North Carolina, for example, an out-of-state applicant who graduates in the top 5 percent of his or her high school class must have combined S.A.T. scores of 1100 to have better than a 50-50 chance of being admitted, while a North Carolina resident in the top 5 percent has a 4 out of 5 chance of being admitted with a combined S.A.T. total of only 800. Whether tougher standards for out-of-state applicants take the form of higher test score requirements (Minnesota), higher grade point averages (Berkeley), or a numerical limit (Vermont), there is usually a double standard of some sort. It is one of many double standards—for athletes, alumni children, ethnic minorities, and others.

In the admissions game, "winning" cannot be defined as simply getting in. At a minimum, it must also include reasonable prospects of survival, and it should of course include more than that. Athletes, ethnic minorities, and alumni children are not the only ones for whom easy admission can turn out to be a trap rather than a favor.

Many private and some state institutions play by a different rule that sets admissions standards at a level that corresponds to some reasonable prospect of successfully completing the academic work. Obviously that level varies from institution to institution but the principle is still pretty straightforward. Complications arise, however, at schools with far more applicants than they can admit. Here the problem is just the opposite of that at many state universities. Here you may be perfectly capable of doing the work and still not be admitted. In this situation it is possible to lose in a number of ways.

The biggest losers in this version of the admissions game are not simply those who are not accepted at prestigious schools they had their hearts set on. It was inevitable from the outset that most would be rejected when the applicants greatly exceeded the places. The real and sometimes lasting harm is that many students take their rejection as a sign of some personal failing, that they didn't "measure up" to a high standard. Many carry the feeling of being a "Stanford reject" or "an Ivy League reject" with them to some other college, which may in fact offer them a better education than they could have gotten at their first-choice institution, and which in any case often has intellectual resources far beyond what anybody can exhaust in four years.

✔ PLAYERS IN THE GAME

The sad irony is that most college admissions committee decisions today bear little resemblance to the process envisioned by students who think that they just didn't "measure up" to some objective academic criteria. With so many applicants with similar academic credentials applying to a relatively few well-known colleges, admissions committees choose on subjective grounds that range from the fashionable to the ideological to the ludicrous.

A student may be favored by a committee member because of personality, interests, or an essay that hits home to the committee member. Some activity that strikes one committee member as exciting and showing initiative—perhaps hitchhiking around Europe in the summer—may strike some other committee member as old stuff, a copycat idea, or even a sign of irresponsibility. Personal meetings between visiting committee members and the student may provide the interest that makes that committee member fight to get that particular student admitted. Or there may just be bad vibes. Scientific it ain't.

Part of any game is knowing what the other players are like. The kind of people on admissions committees varies from institution to institution. However, a world-class phy-

sicist or chemist who is doing pioneering research is unlikely to put it aside, in order to sit on an admissions committee from morning till night, perhaps six or seven days
a week, several weeks in a row, reading application folders.
So, while you may be applying to Harvard or M.I.T. to
study under scholars like that, or in hopes of becoming one
yourself, the people who decide whether or not you get in
are likely to be very different. One study of the admissions
process at Harvard concluded that most Harvard admissions committee members had been neither "brilliant students" themselves nor "truly original and independent"
minds. Yet they are expected to select students with the
very qualities that they themselves lack.

At Harvard as elsewhere, administrators rather than
faculty members tend to predominate on admissions committees. Most tend to be youngish people—often in their
20s—and at best fringe members of the intellectual community. They share, among other things, a belief that they
can discern psychological nuances that matter when choosing among applicants—even though there is not a speck of
evidence that they can. The Harvard admissions committee
is by no means unique in this respect. The college admissions literature in general is full of attempts to play up
amateur psychology and play down academic criteria. This
literature includes persistent and even reckless attempts
to discredit test scores in favor of undefinable qualities like
"leadership," "commitment," and the like. The University
of Virginia admissions brochure, for example, says:

> Recognizing that superior performance and promise do not
> necessarily guarantee success or happiness at any university,
> the Committee tries to understand each applicant in personal
> terms, and accordingly seeks evidence of good character and
> social habits, facility in self-expression, leadership, commit-

ment to service, and any other predictors of positive contributions to the University community.

Obviously, nothing on earth will "guarantee success or happiness"—at a university or anywhere else. It is pathetic that anyone would be shallow enough to use that even as a straw man—much less that such people should control the gateway to an outstanding university. It is equally pathetic that there are grown men and women who seriously believe that they can divine elusive "predictors of positive contributions" (for more than 10,000 applicants, in the case of the University of Virginia). But the cold fact is that such beliefs are widespread—and affect the admissions game. Widespread emphasis on finding evidence of "community service" in the student's application folder is one consequence of this fashionable illusion. At the University of Notre Dame, half of all the students admitted had performed "community service." At Wittenberg University, "community service" is even required for graduation.

Whatever the merits or demerits of amateur psychology applied by admissions committees, and completely aside from whether the various activities under the nebulous label of "community service" are in reality a service or a disservice to the community, the practical fact remains that this is one of the ingredients in the admissions process at many institutions today. It is part of the game. How much weight it carries is unknowable and no doubt varies from institution to institution. However, note that half the people admitted to Notre Dame go in *without* "community service." But the mere fact that this was one of a number of high school "activities" tabulated at Notre Dame shows the general drift. Their brochure points out that more than two-thirds of all Notre Dame freshmen led one or more activities "as President, Captain, or Editor-in-Chief" while in high school.

However impressed some admissions committees may be with this particular conception of "leadership"—which would miss people like Einstein or Beethoven—the cold fact is that millions of students must be admitted to thousands of colleges if those colleges are to survive, and all these students cannot be the ideal applicant, as visualized by admissions committees. How much of your time it is worth investing in scoring points by doing things that look good on an application form is something that only you can decide. If there is some extra-curricular activity that you like for its own sake, then the decision may be easy. If it's just part of a game, then it should be coldly assessed in terms of what it may cost you, by encroaching on your school work, other things you like to do, or perhaps your self-respect. Applying to more colleges to spread the risk from this random factor may be a better use of your time.

With admissions officials, as with other people, it is always a good idea to distinguish what they say from what they do. The admissions office at Carnegie-Mellon University, for example, says: "In our review process, SAT scores take up a very small part of our decision." After various disparagements of S.A.T. scores, including the incredible assertion that these scores are supposed to measure "a fixed and innate quality," the admissions office concludes: "In the long run, the well-rounded student with perhaps the 'average' SAT scores will win out at Carnegie-Mellon." In practice, however, Carnegie-Mellon students' average S.A.T.'s are 300 points above the national average!

Any student with average S.A.T.'s (900 composite) who entered Carnegie-Mellon could be in for a big shock. Data analyzed by Professor Robert Klitgaard of the Kennedy

School at Harvard show that S.A.T. differences of that magnitude have very serious effects on grade-point averages. Always remember that it is not the admissions committee that will flunk out of college if they give you bad advice. Moreover, very few admissions offices make any real effort to collect hard evidence to test any of the fashionable things they say or do. On the contrary, many who have the boldest rhetoric are the most secretive when it comes to preventing any data in their office from being seen by any independent researcher.

Remember, too, when admissions office representatives give talks at your high school, if the representative from some college you respect sounds like a jerk, that does not mean that there is something wrong with the college. Admissions personnel are not necessarily like either the faculty or the students at their institutions. Don't give up on a good college just because its admissions representative sounded shallow. Many of them are.

✔ STRATEGY AND COUNTER-STRATEGY

Once it is understood that getting admitted to college is not strictly a matter of academic qualifications, the whole admissions game can be approached in a different spirit— and its results viewed in a different light. The substantial element of chance means that you must apply to a number of institutions, regardless of how good your academic record may be. Nor should all but one college be regarded as "fall-back" options. It is better to apply to three or four institutions of a very similar academic level and type, with another couple where your chances are greater, and perhaps one "safety valve" school where you feel sure of being admitted, if all else fails. Do not concern yourself at this point with the exact ranking of your choices or about what you will do if you get several acceptances. You can always say "no" but you cannot always say "yes" unless you have left yourself enough options.

Some prefer a strategy of applying to one college a little higher-rated or more "selective" than you might normally expect to be admitted to, followed by those where you meet the usual admissions standards, followed by one or more "safety valve" schools. Despite the symmetry of this approach, and its resemblance to an investment portfolio with diversified risks, I do not share the assumption on which it is based. If getting admitted to a "better" college were a special prize for which it was worth trying, this strategy would make sense. But if a match is better than a mismatch, then the highest academic level of college to apply to is the level whose colleges fit your performance. There is no point trying to "go for the gold" in terms of college prestige rankings, if that will mean four years of struggling to keep your nose above the water.

Counselors and Coaches

Some games require coaches, and college admissions may be one of them, at least for some people. In addition to high school counselors, there are also private coaches of various sorts, charging various amounts of money to coach you on everything from taking S.A.T. tests to taking interviews, writing application essays, and arranging the kinds of extracurricular activities that will appeal to the prejudices and mentality of those who sit on admissions committees. Some of these coaching or counseling services specialize in some aspects more than others but some take on all of them.

Among these coaching services are nationwide organizations like Princeton Review and Stanley H. Kaplan. There are also local coaching and counseling services, such as the College Admissions Preparatory Service (CAPS) on the San Francisco peninsula. The very fact that such organizations can survive and grow, in competition with public schools that provide similar services free of charge, may be a reflection on at least some of the public schools.

I never realized just how bad some public schools can be in this respect until I was sitting in the admissions office at Rockford College with my niece, who attended a ghetto high school in New York. When the admissions officer asked what her S.A.T. scores were, she was baffled because she had never heard of the S.A.T. It had not occurred to me to tell her about it because it had not occurred to me that high school counselors would fail to provide such basic information.

Whether it will be worth your while to find a private coaching and counseling organization will depend on how well your teachers and counselors have done their jobs, and how your academic credentials stack up against the standards of the colleges you are applying to. Even if you meet the normal standards where you are applying, that is far from a guarantee that you will be admitted. The smaller the percentage of applicants a school accepts, the more likely you are to benefit from professional help in packaging your application or in raising your test scores. However, it is well worth remembering that there are many very good colleges that admit more than half of all applicants.

There is a log-jam of applicants to Ivy League schools, M.I.T., Cal Tech, and a relatively few other places, so that the odds are against you there, even if you meet all their standards and are just as able as the students going there now. However, there are many other outstanding institutions—some world class—where things are very different. Nearly half the students who apply to the University of Chicago or to Johns Hopkins are admitted, as are more than half of those who apply to Oberlin, Occidental, or Brandeis.

Even at places where only 20 percent of the applicants are accepted, merely applying to three such places gives you just over a 50-50 chance of getting in at one of them. Applying to six such places would raise the over-all odds to two out of three in your favor. This assumes that you meet the standards, so that it is just the luck of the draw whether you or someone else equally qualified is admitted. Among the institutions where 20 percent or more of the applicants are admitted are M.I.T., Cal Tech, and half the Ivy League, with Harvard and Yale not far behind.

In short, while having the qualifications will not ensure your admissions at any given institution, those qualifications plus half a dozen applications will give you a very good chance of getting into one college at even the most highly selective level. If that is the level you are aiming for, then one or two fall-back applications in addition should cover you. If the colleges you are considering are not at that stratospheric level, meeting the normal standards should be enough to give you a good chance with perhaps five applications. At any level where there are colleges with good academic standards, making less than three applications is taking a needless chance.

In the light of this, the need for a professional counselor may not be urgent. But if you can afford it and have your heart set on one particular place, then perhaps it is a good investment. The other services of a counselor, in coaching you on subjects where you want some beefing up, and in making you aware of possibilities and getting you to think through your own priorities, may be more valuable. But if you cannot afford a private counselor, it is hardly likely to be fatal to your academic future—especially not for those who have read this far.

Essays and Interviews

Among the things professional counselors can help with is preparing the essay which many colleges ask for in their admissions forms and preparing yourself for the interview with an admissions officer.

Ethical questions may arise as to how far someone else should go in helping you prepare an essay that is supposed to be yours. General advice about writing grammatically, avoiding slang, not bringing in controversial issues, and generally being straightforward, is fine. But when the counselor begins to outline the essay for you, you are entering a gray area.

The widespread use of paid counselors by people who can afford it also undermines the easy assumption that admissions committees can discern things that enable them to judge "the whole person." They may in fact be judging a person and a half. What the counselors essentially do in this case is simply enable their client to play the game better—to stand out a little from many other applicants with similar credentials. What makes it a game in the first place is the assumption by admissions committees that they can do something which there is no evidence whatsoever that they can do. While the University of Virginia admissions brochure refers to using "predictors of positive contributions," these are undefined, untested, and unverifiable— not only at Virginia but in general. A vast literature of such vague and lofty expressions can be surveyed at great length without discovering either a single piece of hard evidence or even a basis for testing any of the claims made. There may indeed be things that catch an admissions committee's eye but discovering what they are is essentially a game, whether played alone or with a professional counselor's help.

The college admissions interview may also be a game, though you can make it worthwhile by asking whatever questions you may have about the college and the surrounding community during the interview. With the interview, as with the essay, the best advice is to be straightforward and to be yourself. There is no point being clever with people who have seen thousands of interviewees and have heard all the ploys. Some college guides give a long list of dos and don'ts—followed by the advice to relax! Common sense will tell you not to do outlandish things—and for someone who doesn't have common sense, no list can cover all the ways that that fact will come out.

The advice to relax is good advice for a number of reasons. Perhaps the most important reason is that the interview probably won't make much difference in the admissions decision one way or the other. Some admissions officials themselves say so privately. There may be some other admissions officials who are fatuous enough to think that they can play Sigmund Freud and see deep meaning in a phrase here and a gesture there during an interview. But there is no way to become fool-proof. Applying to a number of colleges is one way of allowing for such risks.

The Colleges' Strategies

In any game, it is well to understand the other players and their strategies and limitations. College admissions officials are generally maximizing the well-being of their institutions, as they define it according to current beliefs, fashions, and conditions. They must, for example, admit far more students than there are places in the freshman class, just as airlines "overbook" flights because they expect "no shows." This is, in effect, the admissions committee's counter-strategy to students' multiple applications to different colleges.

Students feeling admissions pressures as they try to get into the college of their choice should be aware that colleges are also under their own kind of admissions pressure— which is a matter of institutional life or death. For many institutions, it would be a financial disaster not to fill the freshman class or the freshman dormitories. Even colleges with enough surplus applicants to be sure of having enough warm bodies must be concerned to have enough of the "right" kind of students, not only as the admissions committee sees it, but also as the faculty sees it. Even schools with excess applicants, such as Wesleyan and Stanford, are out recruiting as far away as Europe.

Vassar College illustrates the way admissions pressures cut both ways. Just under half the students who apply to Vassar are admitted—but only about a third of those admitted actually enroll. The specific numbers vary from college to college but the general pattern is very similar. Even Yale gets only a little more than half the students it has accepted. Colleges across the country, and across the academic spectrum, have no real choice but to admit far more students than they can handle.

The net effect is to make it easier for a given student to be admitted to a given college, because colleges have been forced to grant more admissions as the practice of multiple applications has spread. This offsets many of the fashions and prejudices of admissions committees as to what an ideal applicant should be. It does not restore aca-

demic criteria but reduces the impact of numerous non-
academic fads, such as "community service" and other extra-curricular criteria.

The students jeopardized by the strategies of admissions committees include many who seem to be favored—
athletes, ethnic minorities, and alumni children. Where
they are admitted without meeting the usual standards,
their survival chances are correspondingly reduced. At
many institutions, the proportion of athletes and minority
students who never graduate is a scandal—and they deserve to be at other institutions which keep these statistics
under lock and key. The effect of special admissions on the
survival rates of alumni children or students with better
"outside activities" and "community service" records than
academic records could stand study as well. The same general principle is involved.

If you are in any of these categories, consider yourself
at risk rather than favored if your academic credentials are
not in the same league as those of the other students at the
college where you are applying. This is one of the dangerous parts of the admissions game.

CHAPTER 12

YOUR CHOICE

After months of waiting and wondering about which college will accept you, the time finally comes when the situation is reversed. After you receive their decisions—and chances are there will be more than one acceptance—you must then decide which of the colleges' admissions offers you will choose to accept.

An acceptance letter, even from a prestigious institution, is not a trophy but a crossroads. However much your friends, relatives, and classmates may be impressed by one acceptance letter and unimpressed by others, it is you who will be living with the consequences of your choice, for years—and decades—to come. If you are accepted by Columbia University and by Davidson College, everyone will congratulate you on the first but many may never have heard of the second. However, at that point, if you have done your homework, you will know far more about both institutions than anyone around you. That knowledge—of the schools and of yourself—should decide for you, not the crowd's reaction.

Income and Career Prospects

What if the graduates of Columbia earn a higher income than the graduates of Davidson? That doesn't mean that *you* are likely to earn a higher income by going to Columbia. My college graduating class undoubtedly has a high average income; it included a Rockefeller and the Agha Khan, among others from wealthy families. But none of that ever added a dime to my income.

Averages are treacherous. Joining a basketball team will not make you any taller, even though the average basketball player is much taller than most people. The average income of its graduates is similarly a very shaky basis for choosing a college.

It would take a complicated analysis—with a very uncertain outcome—to determine how much a given college itself adds to your future income prospects. The field that you major in probably has a much bigger effect. A given individual is unlikely to earn as high an income with a Harvard degree in sociology as with a Georgia Tech degree in engineering.

If your interest is not so much in your prospects immediately after college, but rather in your career after finishing graduate school or medical or law school, then there is even less reason to select a big-name undergraduate institution, as such. The quality and renown of your postgraduate training will undoubtedly have a very real influence on your career prospects—but at that point no one will care where you went to college before you received your M.B.A. from Wharton, your Ph.D. from Stanford, or your M.D. from Johns Hopkins.

Perhaps you are concerned about getting into such postgraduate programs and think that a big-name college will help your chances there. But the people who run the leading graduate and professional institutions are unlikely to be dazzled by big names. They know from long personal experience which colleges' students actually perform well, regardless of whether or not those colleges are known to the general public. It was the deans of law schools who ranked Davidson College ahead of most Ivy League schools for the calibre of its students' performances in law school. It was the deans of engineering schools who ranked the students from Rose-Hulman Institute ahead of those from Princeton.

The Unthinkable

What if the unthinkable happens and you are not admitted to any of the colleges you applied to? This is highly unlikely, unless you made some extremely ill-advised choices. Nevertheless, once it has happened, for whatever reason, what do you do?

Most selective colleges notify you of their decision by mid-April and require you to notify them of your decision by the beginning of May. There are still some respectable institutions to which you can apply by June 1st or later, and still others with "rolling" admissions policies, to which you can apply as long as they have spaces. Among these late-application possibilities are a number of state universities, including California's U.C. Riverside, Michigan State, Purdue, the universities of Nebraska, Kansas, and Iowa; Clemson, Auburn, Colorado State, and others. There are also a number of late-application private institutions, such as Marquette University, Temple University, Wabash College, and Loyola Marymount University. If you are confident that academic credentials will get you in someplace that suits you better next year, perhaps it is better to wait, especially if your problem this year was from applying to too few or too competitive a set of colleges.

If you have not been rejected outright by the college to which you applied, but have been put on the waiting list, then you may need to apply elsewhere to have a fall-back possibility, while sweating out whether you will ultimately be admitted to your preferred college. One of the real dangers in this situation is psychological. If you take being wait-listed personally, you may build up resentments and doubts that may affect your judgment if and when you are finally admitted from the waiting list. Given the chancy nature of the admissions game, there is probably no basis for resentments and doubts—certainly not enough to make it sensible to turn down the admissions offer when it comes.

If the college where you were wait-listed was your preferred choice before, and there is no new information about it, then it should still be your preferred choice. Once you are there, you will be like any other student, including those who received early acceptance. And after you have graduated, being wait-listed is one of the things you can laugh about.

Financial Aid

Money may be a very legitimate concern when it comes to financing your college education, so it is well worthwhile to scrutinize the financial aid offers that come from different colleges. There is no way you can do your best academically if you are going to be constantly hard-pressed to make ends meet, or have to work long hours when you should be studying. When comparing the financial situation as between two colleges, include differences in costs (including travel costs) as well as differences in financial aid.

The financial differences that matter most are those that affect your education while in college. The difference between a campus job and a loan makes a difference in your education. The difference between a loan and a grant does not. Obviously loans will mean that you graduate in debt but being in debt will not affect your life until *after* graduation—and probably not in a major way even then. The difference between a loan and a grant should not be enough to determine your choice if there is a real difference between colleges.

A Choice of Futures

While the admissions process is a game, it is very important to be clear in your own mind as to what "winning" that game means. Some regard acceptance by the most exclusive colleges as "winning." In reality, winning is getting into the college that best matches your particular needs and capabilities. If you succeed in getting into a college whose pace is beyond yours, that can mean losing in a big way.

Your decision at the crossroads is not about right now, but about years from now. This applies to every aspect of the decision, from finances to friendship. It may be tempting to go to a college where your friends are going, but the long-run consequences have to be kept in mind. In the short run, it will be good to know someone the first day you step on a college campus, but chances are you are going to make new friends there anyway. Moreover, these are years when people grow personally and intellectually, by great amounts and in very different directions. That is part of why you go to college. It can be more than ironic to realize in your sophomore or junior year that you chose the wrong college because of someone you seldom spend time with any more.

These are all downside risks. But there are many up sides when you make the right choice. The right college can mean new horizons and a whole new life. Make that choice, not just for the next year or even the next four years, but for the best new life you can find.

ACKNOWLEDGMENTS

I am indebted to more people than I can remember for the information in this book. Much of this information was gathered over years, before there was any thought of writing a book. Some of it was gathered while trying to help particular young people with their own college choices and problems. Because of the potentially controversial nature of this book, I am also reluctant to name individuals who helped me in its preparation. However, there are a number of distinguished institutions whose help in supplying factual material must be acknowledged, though they bear no responsibility for my conclusions.

These institutions include, in alphabetical order, the American College Testing Program; *Change* magazine, which graciously permitted the reprinting of its statistical data*; the College Board; the Office of Institutional Research at Franklin & Marshall College; the National Collegiate Athletic Association; and the National Research Council. In addition, I have benefitted from reading various writings by Mr. Arthur Hu on the admissions of Asian students and have benefitted greatly from reading

*Carol H. Fuller, "Ph.D. Recipients: Where Did They Go to College?" *Change*, vol. 18, no. 6 (November/December, 1986).

Choosing Elites by Professor Robert Klitgaard, a book that should be required reading for anyone who wishes to discuss the predictive validity of tests intelligently, rather than politically.

INDEX

ABOUT THE AUTHOR

Thomas Sowell is a well-known economist, teacher, and lecturer who has taught at U.C.L.A., Amherst, Brandeis, and Cornell, among other schools. He has written extensively on education, economics, and history. Sowell is currently a Senior Fellow of the Hoover Institution at Stanford University and writes a nationally syndicated column for Scripps-Howard.